CONVERSATIONS
WITH SCRIPTURE:

2 ISAIAH

STEPHEN L. COOK

MOREHOUSE PUBLISHING
An imprint of Church Publishing Incorporated
HARRISBURG—NEW YORK

Morehouse Publishing and the Anglican Association of Biblical Scholars thank the Louisville Institute for their interest in and support of this series.

Morehouse Publishing, 4775 Linglestown Road, Harrisburg, PA 17112
Morehouse Publishing, 445 Fifth Avenue, New York, NY 10016
Morehouse Publishing is an imprint of Church Publishing Incorporated.

Cover art by The Rev. Stuart Shelby, St. Martin's Episcopal Church, Houston, Texas
Series design by Beth Oberholtzer

Library of Congress Cataloging-in-Publication Data

Cook, Stephen L., 1962–
    Conversations with Scripture : 2 Isaiah / Stephen L. Cook.
        p.   cm.
    Includes bibliographical references (p.   ) .
    ISBN 978-0-8192-2149-0 (pbk.)
        1. Bible. O.T. Isaiah XL-LXVI—Criticism, interpretation, etc. 2. Spiritual life—Anglican Communion. I. Title.
BS1520.C66   2008
224'.106—dc22
                                                                        2008012717

Printed in the United States of America

06 07 08 09 10   10 9 8 7 6 5 4 3 2 1

For Abigail Hannah Cook

October 31, 2004

"Composed and serene through what she endured,
as if she knew how many loved her."

All Glory be to you, Holy Immortal One, the Holy One of Israel, for you at once both hide yourself in light inaccessible and reveal yourself in history as our Savior. Grant us a spirit of true reverence before you, that we may forsake our pride and embrace each other in other-centered love. You sent your Son, who gave us the example of his great humility: Mercifully grant that we may walk in the way of his selflessness, and also share in his witness to your Majesty, that your salvation may reach to the end of the earth.

AMEN.

Blessed Lord, who caused all holy Scriptures to be written for our learning: Grant us so to hear them, read, mark, learn, and inwardly digest them, that we may embrace and ever hold fast the blessed hope of everlasting life, which you have given us in our Savior Jesus Christ; who lives and reigns with you and the Holy Spirit, one God, for ever and ever.

AMEN.

CONTENTS

Introduction to the Series   vii
Autobiographical Note   xi
Introduction   xv

CHAPTER ONE
Second Isaiah and the Theology of Reverence   1

CHAPTER TWO
The Inscrutability of God in 2 Isaiah   19

CHAPTER THREE
Reverence and the Collapse of Pride and Ignorance   39

CHAPTER FOUR
Servanthood and the Exuberance of the Holy   59

CHAPTER FIVE
Atonement and Exuberance   83

CHAPTER SIX
The Majesty of Servanthood   107

Acknowledgments   131
Study Questions   133
Notes   147
Further Reading   155
About the Author   157

INTRODUCTION
TO THE SERIES

To talk about a distinctively Anglican approach to Scripture is a daunting task. Within any one part of the larger church that we call the Anglican Communion there is, on historical grounds alone, an enormous variety. But as the global character of the church becomes apparent in ever-newer ways, the task of accounting for that variety, while naming the characteristics of a distinctive approach, becomes increasingly difficult.

In addition, the examination of Scripture is not confined to formal studies of the kind addressed in this series of parish studies written by formally trained biblical scholars. Systematic theologian David Ford, who participated in the 1998 Lambeth Conference, rightly noted that although "most of us have studied the Bible over many years" and "are aware of various academic approaches to it," we have "also lived in it" and "inhabited it, through worship, preaching, teaching, and meditation." As such, Ford observes, "The Bible in the Church is like a city we have lived in for a long time." We may not be able to account for the history of every building or the architecture on every street, but we know our way around and it is a source of life to each of us.[1]

That said, we have not done as much as we should in acquainting the inhabitants of that famed city with the architecture that lies within. So, as risky as it may seem, it is important to describe the sights and sounds of the city we call the Bible that matter most to its Anglican residents.

The first of those descriptors that leaps to mind is familiar, basic, and forever debated: *authoritative.* Years ago I was asked by a colleague who belonged to the Evangelical Free Church why someone with as much obvious interest in the Bible would be an Episcopal priest. I responded, "Because we read the whole of Scripture and not just the parts of it that suit us." Scripture has been and continues to play a singular role in the life of the Anglican Communion, but it has rarely been used in the sharply prescriptive fashion that has characterized some traditions.

Some have characterized this approach as an attempt to navigate a *via media* between overbearing control and an absence of accountability. But I think it is far more helpful to describe the tensions not as a matter of steering a course between two different and competing priorities, but as the complex dance necessary to live under a very different, but typically Anglican notion of authority itself. Authority shares the same root as the word "to author" and as such, refers first and foremost, not to the *power* to *control* with all that both of those words suggest, but to the capacity to *author creativity,* with all that both of those words suggest.[2] As such, the function of Scripture is to carve out a creative space in which the work of the Holy Spirit can yield the very kind of fruit associated with its work in the church. The difficulty, of course, is that for that space to be creative, it is also necessary for it to have boundaries, much like the boundaries we establish for other kinds of genuinely creative freedom: the practice of scales for concert pianists, the discipline of work at the barre that frees the ballerina, or the guidance that parents provide for their children. Defined in this way, it is possible to see the boundaries around that creative space as barriers to be eliminated, or as walls that provide protection, but they are neither.

And so the struggle continues with the authority of Scripture. From time to time in the Anglican Communion, it has been and will be treated as a wall that protects us from the complexity of navigating without error the world in which we live. At other times, it will be treated as the ancient remains of a city to be cleared away in favor of a brave new world. But both approaches are rooted, not in the limitations of Scripture, but in our failure to welcome the creative space we have been given.

For that reason, at their best, Anglican approaches to Scripture are also *illuminative.* William Sloane Coffin once observed that the problem with Americans and the Bible is that we read it like a drunk uses a lamppost. We lean on it, we don't use it for illumination.[3] Leaning on Scripture and having the lamppost taken out completely are simply two very closely related ways of failing to acknowledge the creative space provided by Scripture. But once the creative space is recognized for what it is, then the importance of reading Scripture for illumination becomes apparent. Application of the insight Scripture provides into who we are and what we might become is not something that can be prescribed or mapped out in detail. It is only a conversation with Scripture, marked by humility, that can begin to spell out the particulars. Reading Scripture is, then, in the Anglican tradition a delicate and demanding task, that involves both the careful listening for the voice of God and courageous conversation with the world around us.

It is, for that reason, an approach that is also marked by *critical engagement* with the text itself. It is no accident that from 1860 to 1900 the three best-known names in the world of biblical scholarship were Anglican priests, the first two of whom were bishops: B. F. Westcott, J. B. Lightfoot, and F. J. A. Hort. Together the three made contributions to both the church and the critical study of the biblical text that became a defining characteristic of Anglican life.

Of the three, Westcott's contribution, perhaps, best captures the balance. Not only did his work contribute to a critical text of the Greek New Testament that would eventually serve as the basis for the English Revised Version, but as Bishop of Durham he also convened a conference of Christians to discuss the arms race in Europe, founded the Christian Social Union, and mediated the Durham coal strike of 1892.

The English roots of the tradition are not the only, or even the defining, characteristic of Anglican approaches to Scripture. The church, no less than the rest of the world, has been forever changed by the process of globalization, which has yielded a rich *diversity* that complements the traditions once identified with the church.

Scripture in Uganda, for example, has been read with an emphasis on private, allegorical, and revivalist applications. The result has been a tradition in large parts of East Africa that stresses the reading of Scripture on one's own: the direct application made to the contemporary situation without reference to the setting of the original text; and the combination of personal testimony with the power of public exhortation.

At the same time, however, globalization has brought that tradition into conversation with people from other parts of the Anglican Communion, as the church in Uganda has sought to bring the biblical text to bear on its efforts to address the issues of justice, poverty, war, disease, food shortage, and education. In such a dynamic environment, the only thing that one can say with certainty is that neither the Anglican Communion, nor the churches of East Africa, will ever be the same again.

Authoritative, illuminative, critical, and varied—these are not the labels that one uses to carve out an approach to Scripture that can be predicted with any kind of certainty. Indeed, if the word *dynamic* is added to the list, perhaps all that one can predict is still more change! But such is the nature of life in any city, including one shaped by the Bible. We influence the shape of its life, but we are also shaped and nurtured by it. And if that city is of God's making, then to force our own design on the streets and buildings around us is to disregard the design that the chief architect has in mind.

—Frederick W. Schmidt
Series Editor

AUTOBIOGRAPHICAL NOTE

Two wonderful teachers of Bible at Trinity College, Connecticut, both Episcopalians, first stimulated my fascination with 2 Isaiah (i.e., Isaiah 40–66). Dr. John A. Gettier worked with me patiently, one-on-one, reading Isaiah's Hebrew, carefully parsing its parallel lines and unpacking its rich, pregnant language. Dr. Theodore Mauch immersed me in 2 Isaiah in a somewhat different mode. During his semester-long seminar on Isaiah 40–55, a group of about a dozen of us undergraduates wrestled communally with Isaiah's texts, especially with their rhetorical and poetic form and with their thinking and vision of life.

In Dr. Mauch's classroom, the emphasis on reverence in 2 Isaiah, which I explore in this book, came to life. Together with our teacher, we found ourselves reverent—in awe before the beauty and depth of the Scriptures before us. Isaiah's texts were constantly repaying our close inspection of their details, rewarding our probing at their truths. Before these magnificent compositions, students and professor labored together, in respect and mutuality, working to better understand something that captivated, amazed, and humbled us all.

Dr. Mauch had the calm wisdom and "disciple's tongue" of 2 Isaiah's Suffering Servant (Isa 50:4). He empowered his students to plumb the Bible's depths for ourselves, since he truly respected us. Rarely lecturing at us, he was constantly beside us as a fellow learner instead—sitting with us around a big wooden table, joining with us in our study of the seemingly inexhaustible riches of 2 Isaiah's poems. Ted Mauch died August 18, 2007, while this book was in its final stages of preparation. May his memory be a blessing.

At Trinity College we read the Bible with diligence and care. The stress on detailed study and patient rumination that I learned there finds strong resonances in a venerable Anglican tradition of studying the Bible. The great Anglican reformer Thomas Cranmer wrote to all the English churches, "Let us ruminate, and, as it were, chew the cud, that we may have the sweet juice, spiritual effect, marrow, honey, kernel, taste, comfort and consolation" of the Scriptures.[1] Words to similar effect appear in Cranmer's beautiful Collect on Holy Scriptures, which I have included above, immediately before the Table of Contents.

Whereas in college, as a religion major, I learned to love Hebrew and detailed exegetical research, it was later during my divinity and doctoral studies at Yale that I began to develop skills in theological interpretation and hermeneutics. At Yale I learned rigorous, defensible approaches for exploring the Bible *as the Scripture of the church.* These approaches have been an invaluable resource for me to this day, especially in my current duties of preparing Episcopal seminarians for ministry.

Studying with geniuses at Yale, such as Brevard S. Childs, I learned to approach the Bible along the lines of an Anglican *via media,* steering a "middle way" between positions in opposition within the church's experience. Such a *via media* is crucial in our day, as we confront great polar tensions and culture wars both in society and in the Anglican Communion. Many of these highly charged tensions revolve directly around differing understandings of how to approach the Bible.

Taking a *via media* in studying the Scriptures means avoiding two extremes, one on the right and one on the left. On the right, the danger is that of being anti-hermeneutical, of discounting the necessity of grappling with the Bible's ancient, alien context, which bars us from what one might call "bare readings."

We must appreciate the immense historical distance between us and the Bible's first audience. We must practice informed, judicious moderation in applying ancient, alien words today. As the great Anglican theologian Richard Hooker stated, "bare reading" of Scripture provides only "bare feeding" for hungry souls.[2]

Heeding Hooker's warning, this book takes the ancient, alien context of 2 Isaiah seriously. Like a good archaeologist, I strive to date the Isaiah authors' activity and identify their sources. I unearth our texts' writers and their context, identifying them as Aaronide priests living in Babylonian exile. I excavate their unique, priestly way of thinking, which is so foreign to contemporary, secular patterns of thought.

On the left, there is a battle to be fought as well. There are real dangers to be faced, especially the risk of discounting the spiritual *vitality* of scriptural traditions. Modernist interpreters too often downplay the Bible's character as an inspired, revealed witness to the reality of God. This is a mistake, for our texts' inspired witness— their *kerygmatic* power—is what accounts for their preservation as sacred Scripture. It was because the ancient faith community valued biblical traditions as power-laden Word, producing fruit, performing God's purposes (Isa 55:11), that the faithful treasured and archived them as *canonical* texts.

This front in the culture wars must be diligently defended. Thus, I take special pains to show the profound impact of priestly Scriptures from the Pentateuch on 2 Isaiah's prophecies. I demonstrate that texts such as Leviticus 10:3 never remained moored in the past, buried in ancient Israel's history. Alive with vitality, such texts demonstrably animated the theology and proclamation of 2 Isaiah.

As we study 2 Isaiah, you will feel the powerful background influence of the demand of God in Leviticus 10:3: "Through those who are near me I will show myself holy, and before all the people I will be glorified." This Word plainly exercised incontrovertible power and authority over our priestly, exilic authors. Its intrinsic weightiness gave it, like many other biblical traditions, a self-authenticating claim. It staked a claim to belong to the emerging corpus of Israel's Scriptures, those Scriptures that we now call the Bible.

INTRODUCTION

The "Holy One of Israel," the God of 2 Isaiah, is increasingly foreign to modern Anglicans. We balk at the uncanny, fiery side of God. Unfortunately, this leaves us frustrated both with God's "non-rational" ways and with our morality-centered Christianity. To find any real peace of mind and spirit, today's church needs to reacquaint itself with the awesome writings that I treat in this book, writings that give us a direct entrée into the idea of the Holy, the idea of the radical mystery and otherness of divinity.

The new research behind this book reveals 2 Isaiah as priestly, temple literature, expert at the Holy and its coming dawn on earth. 2 Isaiah knows the priestly themes to highlight and the temple texts to quote for a blessed communion with the inexpressible, the utterly mysterious. To study this material is to rediscover the overwhelming, absolute worth of God.

Entering 2 Isaiah's world, we immediately experience awe, creaturely humility, and submergence before God's overwhelming presence. Be forewarned: this experience will almost certainly disorient and challenge you. It is nothing other than discovering that all your hard-earned competence, wisdom, and mastery is trivial, a mere drop of water in an endless sea.

The theologian Karl Rahner illustrates it this way. He describes human knowledge as a mere tiny island in a vast, terrifying ocean. All of our medicine, science, and scholarship taken together give us but a small lamp that helps us make our way around our island home. When we stand at the shore and look out at the sea, however, we realize that our little lamp is of practically no value.

The sea in Rahner's metaphor is the sheer, towering loftiness of the realm of the Holy, the transcendent. Faced with this sea, standing before the irreducible, incomprehensible mystery of God, the human soul is impelled to make a profound choice. "Which does he love more, the small island of his so-called knowledge or the sea of infinite mystery? Is the little light with which he illuminates this island . . . to be an eternal light which will shine forever for him? That would surely be hell."[3]

The theme of the tremendousness of God has immediate relevance to readers in the parish. Given our experience of suffering in the world, and in many of our personal lives, it is natural to question and criticize God's ways in the manner of the protests of Job. God exists and God cares, 2 Isaiah claims, but God's uncanny ways sometimes defy our human categories of rationality and morality. We humans need to think of God with more imagination, spiritually oriented on the *otherness* of God.

Not surprisingly, 2 Isaiah's theme of God's mystery and hiddenness has been a powerful resource for some Jewish theologians wrestling with God's absence during the Nazi Holocaust, when millions of Jews died in the death camps.[4] Though it defies normal rationality, Isaiah claims God's self-concealing nature is in itself salvific. God saves *by means of* God's hiddenness: "Truly, you are a God who hides himself, O God of Israel, *the Savior*" (Isa 45:15, emphasis added).

If this paradox of Isaiah is true, as I will argue it is, then the Holocaust is evidence neither of a nonexistent God nor of a God who willingly inflicts senseless punishments on God's people. God did not forsake God's people during the Nazi era. The horrors of this era, however, push us back to 2 Isaiah in our need for the comfort of God's spirit and for growth in our spiritual understanding.

The sense of frailty before a holy God that 2 Isaiah evokes lays the groundwork for a further spiritual move: abandoning self-concern and embracing a lifestyle of servanthood. The true servant of God, according to Isaiah's texts, moves beyond preoccupation with the self, and the present lot of the self, to embrace a kind of self-transcendence. Transcending the self, true servants of the Lord turn outward in love toward the other, that is, toward the neighbor.

This kind of servant-love is purely for the sake of the neighbor, not any ulterior motive. Though one might think that such a lifestyle would debase and nullify the self, 2 Isaiah makes the opposite claim. Paradoxically, the radical lifestyle these texts depict ends up with the self affirmed and blessed, exalted not nullified.

A model, ideal servant of the Lord emerges before our eyes in 2 Isaiah: the Lord's *Suffering Servant*. This enigmatic figure mysteriously accomplishes an amazing work of atonement on behalf of earth's people. God is making all things new, according to 2 Isaiah, preparing to reveal the glory of the Lord before all flesh, and the preparation involves the decisive work of this suffering hero. Though unattractive, despised, and apparently smitten of God, this figure turns out to be the most important individual and truest friend one could ever know.

God's Suffering Servant is far different from earth's proud tyrants, but in his own unique way manifests a beauty of God that shuts kings' mouths and makes princes fall prostrate. The Suffering Servant displays the *majesty* of the Holy, and those of us who choose to follow in his footsteps are expected to do so as well. God wants each of us joyfully to bear the *image of God*, the dignified role of God's regents over earth.

Bearing royal beauty sounds unfamiliar and suspect, and there is real spiritual danger in the thought. As Saint Aelred of Rievaulx (1110–1167 CE) puts it, "If any creature should desire to be like God, in a way that God cannot approve, it is made by that very desire less like God."[5] Nevertheless, despite the danger, we must take the notion of bearing God's majesty seriously.

St. Aelred also states that through the self-sacrifice of Jesus Christ, "The image of God within us is perfectly reformed."[6] If this is true, we cannot imagine we can practice servanthood quietly and privately, keeping God's image under wraps. A lifestyle of divine grace will attract public attention. According to 2 Isaiah, God plans to use it in bringing about the necessary end of history, namely, the union of all people into one great family of God.

CHAPTER ONE

Second Isaiah and the Theology of Reverence

Concentrate on your breathing and pay no heed to your lightheadedness. Ignore your clammy palms and the cold sweat soaking your clothes. Those goose bumps on your skin, the shivers up your back, and the quaking of your knees are just a fluke. It is only the book of Isaiah, right? It is only a mere Old Testament prophet, approved for general audiences—or, did they get that wrong?

Isaiah's God is the safe companion and gentle shepherd we have always imagined—or, are we sure?

What if we experience in reading the book of Isaiah—perhaps for the first time in our lives—a spine-tingling encounter with the uncanny *otherness* of God? What if Isaiah imparts to us, its readers, true knowledge of what religious thinkers like to call "the Holy"? Then, in studying Isaiah, we would be in for a serious engagement with the towering self-existent being of God.

Brace yourself, because you *are* in for just such an engagement in the pages you are about to read. In meditating on Isaiah's prophecies, encountering Isaiah's holy God, you will be aiming a steady gaze at the "high and lofty one who inhabits eternity, whose name is Holy" (Isa 57:15). So prepare for smarting eyes and a spinning head. To proceed farther is to put one's self and one's lifestyle of comfort at risk.

Holiness: The Otherness of God

Presently, I shall introduce you to the book of Isaiah and its contents. But, first things first. Have you met Isaiah's God?

Throughout Isaiah, God goes by the name "Holy One of Israel." The word "holy" in the Bible (Hebrew *kadosh*) has less to do with moral excellence than with radical separation and hiddenness. To be holy is to exist apart from and be *other* than the creation. To put it plainly, God's holiness is all about God's *otherness*.

Kadosh: the Hebrew word for "holy," meaning that which is radically separate and other.

Characteristically, Isaiah's Lord asks, "To whom will you liken me and make me equal, and compare me, as though we were alike?" (Isa 46:5). The question is rhetorical, the answer obvious. The God of Isaiah is matchless, incomparable, and radically *other*. "There is no other," God declares in Isaiah 46:9, "there is no one like me." In Isaiah's celebrated vision of God in Jerusalem's temple (Isa 6), the Lord is surrounded by flaming creatures. Do you recall what they are they saying? They cry to one another, "Yahweh is Other! Other! Other!" (my translation).

The God we meet in reading Isaiah is unlike anyone or anything else we know, whether in the world around us or in the dazzling films we see in our theaters. God's awesome, compelling otherness encounters us head on in the prophecies of Isaiah.

We barely have the images or concepts to imagine divine holiness, Isaiah's God is so awesomely other. As God, God's self, declares, "As the heavens are higher than the earth, so are my ways higher than your ways and my thoughts than your thoughts" (Isa 55:9). This deity is as far removed from an Einstein as from an amoeba. The Lord's otherness is immeasurable. In unapproachable light, separated from us by an infinite gulf, Isaiah's God dwells apart from the world.

Silence! Hush! Reading the book of Isaiah and encountering Isaiah's God, we clam up. We stand in awe, taken aback—disoriented (Isa 52:15). We feel exposed and conscious of our profaneness, yet captivated and impelled to experience more. True holiness is not only daunting but also uniquely fascinating and entrancing. It even inspires self-surrender—indeed, rapture.

What is this holy God up to? According to Isaiah's book, God's endgame is a tangible dawning of holiness on earth. As the goal of history, God's holy presence will physically shine on God's people for the entire world to see. When this happens, the nations of earth will finally recognize the truth of God, and they will worship. "The LORD will arise upon you, and his glory will appear over you. Nations shall come to your light, and kings to the brightness of your dawn. Lift up your eyes and look around; they all gather together, they come to you," God declares to daughter Zion (Isa 60:2–4).

The church today often appears myopically focused on preaching and teaching about day-to-day living, not on this advent. Isaiah would believe we are missing our calling as a consequence. Instead of offering techniques for living healthy lives, Isaiah would have us tenaciously direct the nations' attention toward the dawning of the sacred on earth. God's claim in Isaiah is unambiguous: "I am coming to gather all nations and tongues; and they shall come and shall see my glory" (Isa 66:18). Are we serious about this claim?

Appreciating the Virtue of Reverence

The challenge of knowing God in God's otherness is as relevant now as it was at the book of Isaiah's first appearance two and a half millennia ago. Now, as then, we are finite, dependent mortals, able to grasp our significance only by coming to know the one who fashioned us in the divine image. Still today, just as in biblical times, knowing God is crucial to knowing ourselves, our place in existence, and our destiny.

We are finite, dependent mortals, able to grasp our significance only by coming to know the one who fashioned us in the divine image.

Knowing God is also crucial to becoming more humane persons, aware of our finitude and need of each other. This brings us to the topic of reverence. To encounter God's holiness is to savor a taste of *reverence,* a crucial virtue but one that is almost forgotten these days. We in the global north have largely lost reverence, which we can define as the capacity for awe at those things truly greater than ourselves, which we cannot change, or control, or fully understand. We have lost our capacity for the one virtue uniquely capable of reminding us of our mortality, of binding humanity together in mutuality and compassion.

Reverence is about much more than just being serious during ceremonial rites and church liturgies. It expresses itself strongly in respect for the human dignity of our neighbors and for the wonders of the natural world. We tend to value even the lowly and the marginalized among us when we come to acknowledge that we share with them a common human frailty and ignorance. We begin to shudder at the thought of desecrating the environment when we realize that we cannot control what will happen if we do.

Reverence: the capacity for awe at those things truly greater than ourselves, which we cannot change, or control, or fully understand.

Awe before Isaiah's God refreshes our reverence. It submerges the ego, paving the way for owning up to our frailty. It turns us outward from concern with self to the need and suffering of others, especially the poor and peripheral. As we repose ever more deeply in God's mystery, the Lord who is absolutely sufficient for our succor increasingly works through us to relieve others' brokenness. Simultaneously, the Holy transforms us into ever more reverent advocates of the natural world.

Introducing the Book of Isaiah

Isaiah is one of the biggest books in the Bible (1,292 verses), and one of its greatest. As we shall see, it is among the richest and most theologically profound of the Scriptures. Because Isaiah affords God's people absolute basics of the faith, the book has long been a favorite of both synagogue and church. From the beginnings of Judaism and Christianity, the faithful have granted Isaiah's book a large presence in their lives. Copies of Isaiah were most numerous among the documents of the Dead Sea Scroll community at Qumran. Along with the Psalms, Isaiah is the most quoted biblical book in the New Testament.

Today, we hear Isaiah in church on Sundays more than any other biblical prophet (fifty separate readings all told). That is about as much as all the other prophetic books combined (fifty-five readings).

Qumran: the ancient settlement site of the early Jewish sect associated with the Dead Sea Scrolls.

Just as the faithful have long treasured Isaiah, they have also long wrestled with the book's diverse contents and with the variety of eras it treats. The problem of the origins and dating of its several parts has proved particularly vexing. Struggle over Isaiah's authorship has been especially agonizing and divisive for the church in modern times. Let me briefly explain the situation.

Isaiah, the prophet whose name the book bears, exercised a powerful ministry in Jerusalem, the capital of Israel's southern kingdom of Judah, between 740 and 700 BCE. At his time, the major superpower in the Near East was the empire of Assyria, which posed a daunting military threat to the entire region, preoccupying Judah's leaders. The last twenty-seven chapters of the book of Isaiah, however, concern a later era, after Isaiah's time. Their backdrop is a world dominated by two new superpowers, the empires of Babylonia and Persia.

BCE and CE: "Before the Common Era" and "Common Era." These terms have replaced BC and AD, respectively, within most scholarly circles.

The later chapters of Isaiah revolve around an imminent homecoming of Judah's leaders from an exile in Babylonia, which was imposed by King Nebuchadnezzar of Babylon in two stages from 597 to 586 BCE. They spotlight the advent from about 550 BCE of the Persian ruler Cyrus the Great, whose forces defeated Babylonia and made the homecoming possible, and they wrestle with faithful living in a restored Judah in the wake of the people's return.

Just because a biblical book covers a broad time frame does not prove it had multiple authors. This is especially true of a book of prophecy, where visionary perception is at play. Prophecy claims to discern the course of the future and to speak plainly about it. In Isaiah's case, however, we have a book with two parts that for all the world appear to come from two separate eras of history. Strong clues uncovered by rigorous spadework reinforce the suggestion that the book really did only reach its present form after centuries of writing, more writing, and editing.

Not everyone agrees on when to date Isaiah's two major parts, but they do agree that chapters 40–66 represent a major new departure compared to chapters 1–39. Isaiah's second part looks forward with exuberance to God's imminent salvation. It is full of messages of comfort and hope. It specifically addresses the challenges involved in the homecoming of Judah's Babylonian exiles. With its emphasis on joy and the fulfillment of hopes, Isaiah 40–66 is the special *gospel* section of Isaiah's book. Here we find the Scriptures that make Isaiah the great communicator of the Good News of salvation in the Old Testament.

Orienting Ourselves to 2 Isaiah

Let us concentrate on Isaiah's second part (Isa 40–66), which for convenience we may call *2 Isaiah.* In these chapters we find the culmination and fulfillment of all of Isaiah's prophecies, where God's holy *otherness* finally appears manifest on earth. Here, Isaiah's theology of reverence comes into its own.

One of the first questions you may want answered about Isaiah 40–66 concerns authorship. Who wrote 2 Isaiah, if not Isaiah of Jerusalem?

2 Isaiah was set down in writing by a community of Babylonian exiles who were followers of Isaiah. The community worked in the tradition of its group founder, Isaiah of Jerusalem, upholding the same reverence-oriented theology that he did. There was no so-called anonymous Babylonian refugee who, according to some books and commentaries you may have seen, single-handedly authored our texts. By the end of this chapter you will see why this must be so.

What were the beliefs and values of this community? Where were its members coming from in terms of their thinking and their spirituality?

The community of 2 Isaiah treasured specific theological traditions, which they inherited from their forebears. These sources of their thinking lie in priestly portions of Genesis, Exodus, and other books at the start of the Bible (texts such as Gen 1:1–2:4; Gen 17; Exod 7:8–13; and Lev 5:14–6:7). We must deal with these texts if we are ever to understand the message of the group.

Reverence School: a source of the Pentateuch, originating in priestly circles, which stresses divine otherness and the virtue of reverence.

In what follows, let us agree to refer to these source documents of 2 Isaiah as texts of the *Reverence School.* ("RS" can serve as an abbreviation for the school's writings.) Why do I suggest this title, emphasizing the word "reverence"? Because, at its core, the Reverence School stresses God's hiddenness and otherness, just as 2 Isaiah does.

Think of the Reverence School as a source of the Pentateuch (the first five books of the Bible). It is a strand of priestly texts running through these so-called Books of Moses. Over time, editors combined such sources or strands to produce the Bible's core Scriptures, Genesis through Deuteronomy.

It is easy to see the themes of divine *otherness* and human *reverence* in this source. The texts of the Reverence School strenuously avoid speaking of God in human terms ("anthropomorphism"), as if God made a home in the temple or consumed sacrificial offerings. Israel plays no part in satisfying God's needs, the school insists, and must never bring meal or drink offerings inside the temple building lest they convey such an impression (Exod 30:9). The people must never imagine that God is hungry or thirsty, like the anthropomorphic idols of Canaan and Mesopotamia.

According to the Reverence School, God's otherness is apparent from our human feelings of vulnerability and impurity in response to our experiences of God. For example, this source assumes that God's worshipers feel profane and unclean in God's presence, in desperate need of atonement (Lev 1:4). Sometimes, despite being unaware of any specific transgression, God's people have an overpowering consciousness of guilt (Lev 5:17–19).

Related to such feelings of worshipers are certain instincts of priests, particularly the instinct to keep "covered" in performing God's service. The priests of the Reverence School feel exposed and vulnerable in their sacred duties at the temple, and so wear special vestments and practice protective rituals, such as being dabbed and sprinkled with oil and blood (Lev 8).

By emphasizing rituals of atonement and priestly consecration, our texts put forward reverence as the sole appropriate response to God. Any other attitude is a complete affront, as is apparent from God's decree: "By those who come near me I will be treated as holy, and before all the people I will be honored" (Lev 10:3 NASB).

> By those who come near me I will be treated as holy, and before all the people I will be honored. —Lev 10:3 NASB

According to the Reverence School, God does not dwell on earth, or in the temple as in a house, but at times makes spectacular epiphanies in the world. During such appearances, the transient spectacle of the "glory of the LORD" reveals

God's presence in fire, light, and smoke (Exod 24:15–18; Lev 10:2). When God steps out like this, it is very hard to miss. People fall on their faces, prostrate in reverence (Lev 9:23–24; cf. Isa 40:5). Even Aaron, Israel's premier priest, can do nothing but fall silent on such an occasion (Lev 10:3).

The fiery glory of God is dangerous to humans, according to the Reverence School—in fact, it is lethal. When God's otherness blazes forth in space and time, it consumes the sacrilegious (Lev 10:2). To be safe, Israel must make a thorough atonement in preparation for such an event (Lev 9:6–7, 23–24; cf. Isa 40:2). The regimens of the temple sanctuary and its priests are crucial in preparing to encounter the Lord.

The Reverence School's concerns go far beyond maintaining the temple precincts and keeping worshipers safe from God's burning otherness. Beginning with the majestic story of the cosmos' beginnings in Genesis 1, the school's Scriptures narrate the course of a unique divine intention to bless creation. The more we read, the more we become convinced that this special blessing will progress toward fulfillment despite all obstacles, despite every stubborn human resistance.

As we begin to read the writings of 2 Isaiah, we shall see God's intention to bring blessing to earth materialize before our eyes. 2 Isaiah's prophecies describe the fulfillment of the hopes of the Reverence School. They proclaim the ultimate in Good News.

Guidelines for Reading Prophetic Literature

2 Isaiah is a body of Hebrew *prophecy,* and readers expecting another genre, such as prayers, self-help, or history lessons, are in for frustration. Prophecy is divine word channeled through human messengers, aimed at a target audience. Its words are revelatory, confronting humanity with the reality of God, challenging alternative realities. Such words are dynamic, setting in motion God's will for weal or woe on earth, summoning a human response. As the "rain and the snow," sent by God, "return not again, but water the earth, bringing forth life and giving growth," so God's prophetic word "will not return . . . empty." God declares that this word will assuredly "accomplish that which I have purposed" (Episcopal *Book of Common Prayer,* Canticle 10, Isa 55:6–11).

Rarely verbose or long-winded, the classical Hebrew prophets employed a terse, dense style of communication. They delivered pointed, well-crafted words of promise, indictment, threat, and command. Their books of prophecies, as we now have them in Scripture, thus represent a medley of compact, targeted messages. These messages are sometimes blunt, sometimes subtle; they are caustic here, comforting there. Do not expect them to be consistent with one another in perspective, tone, or detail. It is doubtful that ancient Hebrew prophets and modern systematic theologians, if placed in the same room, would get along.

If you are new to Hebrew prophecy, you should probably try to approach 2 Isaiah as a collection, that is, an anthology. Unlike some anthologies, there is unity, method, and organization to this collection, but it is far from the seamless writing with a smooth, coherent flow that you may have been expecting. Be prepared for breaks in continuity and even some jerky transitions.

I should qualify these points. The prophecies of 2 Isaiah are dense and rich, as I have said, but they constitute more extended discourses than earlier oracles in Israel's history. Here, prophecy has developed beyond earlier, simpler forms into longer compositions with multiple, interlinked segments, vivid scenes, lyrical interludes, and allusions to preceding Scriptures, in particular those of the Reverence School. And Isaiah's organization appears more intricate, and its argument more cumulative, than that of many preceding prophetic books.

Oral qualities, like those of earlier prophecies, are present in 2 Isaiah, and some people have imagined that its words were first sermons, at home in synagogue-like settings in Babylonian exile. The prophecies' well-developed composition, however, suggests their authors fashioned them from the start as writings and circulated them as such, without any initial oral delivery. In fact, 2 Isaiah may well have arisen as an appendix or literary supplement to First Isaiah.

Poetry as a Vehicle of Reverence

No introduction to 2 Isaiah would be close to adequate without discussing its magnificent poetry. Many of Israel's prophets used poetics to express their messages, but the compositions of 2 Isaiah are mas-

Parallelism: the tendency within Hebrew poetry to "double back" to preceding thoughts and wordings so as to balance, second, or intensify meaning and expression.

terworks of art—a pinnacle of biblical expression. Its authors are literary geniuses, preeminent in their skill at poetic parallelism, allusion, exclamation, onomatopoeia, and many other rhetorical devices.

Isaiah's poetic power relates directly to its authors' unique capacity for awe at God's otherness. The purring engine directly below their writing is the sheer ecstasy of encountering the Holy. With pure reverence below the hood, lyrical energy literally throbs in Isaiah's pages.

Repeatedly in 2 Isaiah, hymns celebrate the dawning of the sacred on earth. Joy-filled reverence bursts off the page, for example, in the twenty-third verse of chapter 44:

> [23] Sing, O heavens, for the LORD has done it; /
> shout, O depths of the earth; //
> break forth into singing, O mountains, /
> O forest, and every tree in it! //
> For the LORD has redeemed Jacob, /
> and will be glorified in Israel. //[1]

In a visionary experience, our authors' enraptured eyes have witnessed God's coming in world history and they can barely contain their reverence. It surges through their souls. Now I ask you: How can some commentators assert that 2 Isaiah is merely about earthly politics—exile and repatriation? Even if surrounded by irreverence, a reader cannot help but sense awe here. What will it be like for God to show forth the divine glory, displaying it through Israel like a magnificent crown jewel? Creation itself will don choir robes and belt out praise. A triple-decker choir, their strains will stream forth from three stories: the heavens, the earth, and the under-earth.

The joy will extend from the heights to the depths of creation, as the parallel sections of the first line declare. By setting forth both its extremes, the parallelism drives home how the entire cosmos will burst with joy. Heavens, raise the roof! Sheol, wake the dead! Let loose with praise, for God's glory appears in all its otherness!

Then, the focus moves to the surface of the earth, humanity's home. Earth's majestic mountains, its pride and glory, join in the cosmic refrain. Corresponding to their song is the parallel praise of the forests, which cover the natural world with shade and beauty. Every species is included, from oaks to pines to cedars. Indeed, not a single larch or willow declines to participate.

Amazingly, our poem's artistry gives readers the very sounds of reverence. Take the command to the mountains to sing, for example. As one pronounces the Hebrew words, air first bursts noisily through a narrowing in the vocal tract. Then, a soulful joy rings out expressively through successive *r*-sounds. Finally, resonances echo forth as the lips, tongue, and palate voice a series of *m*'s and *n*'s. The art of onomatopoeia has supplied us with rich Hebrew sounds of reverence.

Fanning the Embers of Reverence

Cultivating a capacity for awe is far from easy. One strains to find ways to help people move toward reverence if they lack much experience with it. What can help is fiery poetry. Its flames may rekindle the embers of reverence yet smoldering in most people's hearts. Isaiah 45:14c–15, another fine snippet from 2 Isaiah's poems, aims to do precisely that.

In the larger context of this snippet, several African nations have just approached the restored exiles, now home on Mount Zion. They have had an epiphany: Israel's God is the one and only Lord. Their awestruck words, which they address to Zion and her restored children, are the ones in quotation marks.

> [14c] They will make supplication to you, saying, /
>   "God is with you alone, and there is no other; /
>   there is no god besides him." //
> [15] Truly, you are a God who hides himself, /
>   O God of Israel, the Savior. //

Verse 15 immediately grabs our attention. Its declaration of God's self-concealment bears a striking similarity to an Egyptian hymn praising the deity Amun, the "hidden one," the "invisible one." This allusion to Amun in our poem powerfully communicates the idea of the Holy to an audience in desperate need of a rekindled spirit of reverence.

Amun: "the hidden one"; a deity in ancient Egyptian mythology.

Amun was familiar to Israelite audiences (cf. Jer 46:25). Our text's subtle echo of his nature is poetic

genius, for it supplies an immediate handle on the ineffable otherness of the true God, Yahweh. It is hard to grasp the nature of the
Holy without such a point of contact.

Our poem provides its readers with a keen "aha" moment. The
Lord—"a God who hides himself" (v. 15)—is like Amun, the Egyptian god who is forever "hiding himself."[2] Amun is hidden indeed, his
Egyptian hymn declares. His being is permanently removed from
any reality with which we are in touch. Shrouded in a cloud of
unknowing, Amun is "one whose identity is hidden, inasmuch as it
is inaccessible."

Even the other gods, Amun's hymn announces, are completely in
the dark about Amun's true nature. "No god knows his true appearance." He dwells concealed. He is "deeper than the Duat," that is, he
is beyond the Underworld.

Our poem gives its readers a handle on holiness and awe, but it
does not stop there. It alludes to Amun, but then gets its readers
thinking about the unique grace of the Lord, Isaiah's God. The Lord
exercises hiddenness in a way that will change everything for the
better. The Lord goes about holiness in a way that will leave all other
gods in the dust. Amun's type of hiddenness is limiting: it isolates
him from any direct impact on the world. He is "too great to investi-
gate, too powerful to know." Sadly, Amun is simply too holy to be
relevant. Not so with the Lord, Yahweh!

The Lord is on the move to display holiness on the stage of world
history. Specifically, God is rolling out the red carpet before King
Cyrus of Persia, guiding him to liberate Israel and others besides.
The Egyptians, the Ethiopians, and the Sabeans have watched the
unfolding drama. Fully captivated, they have made pilgrimage to
Zion. Their praise of God's *otherness* is central to our poem.

Amun is paralyzed by his hiddenness, but the Lord is stepping
out, primed for action. God's ways are impossible to foresee, expres-
sive of utter freedom. Strange is his deed! Alien is his work! Who
could ever have imagined that Israel would owe its restoration to a
reverent pagan, Cyrus the Great? That's a kind of hiddenness that
makes a difference in the world; that's holiness with impact!

With their hands folded in reverence, the nations quietly confess
amazement at God in verse 14. Far from cowering in terror, they

are wondrously, joyously spellbound. Here is another difference from Amun. The wonder-filled fascination of these African peoples is nothing like the stultifying horror that Amun inspires. According to his hymn, Amun's nature spells only danger and confusion. "Instantaneously falling face to face into death is [the fate decreed] for the one who expresses [Amun's] secret identity, unknowingly or knowingly."

After reading Isaiah's poetry, one balks at this limited grasp that Amun's followers had of the Holy. Reverence for deities like Amun, associated only with feelings of terror, is lopsided and tragic. Amun's devotees have missed the dual character of the Holy: its potential for blissful ravishment as well as ghastly horror.

True holiness *saves*. Verse 15 of our poem leaves no doubt about this. The verse, which begins by stressing God's mystery, mounts to a remarkable climax in the word "Savior." Verse 15 is a model line of Hebrew poetry, with two parallel sections interacting dynamically. The sections balance each other, inviting us to ponder the paradox of their complementarity. God "hides himself," the first section declares; God is "the Savior," the second responds. Our poem's artistry asks us to consider how these assertions interrelate. How does God's hiddenness end up spelling salvation?

HOW TRUE HOLINESS SAVES

Our poem directly juxtaposes God's otherness with God's saving power, challenging us to consider their interconnection. Take a minute to puzzle this out with me. I suggest that the key to understanding this mysterious pairing is the magnetic—dare I say *erotic*?—pull of the Holy.

The Holy yanks the human ego away from self-preoccupation. Pulled in by its embrace, the human soul is submerged in God's vastness, ravished before pure tremendousness. Liberated from selfishness, the soul reaches out beyond anything holding it in, grasping for intimacy with other earthbound mortals.

Cyrus the Great made a step in this direction in a story related by the ancient historian Herodotus (ca. 484–425 BCE). Once as he was witnessing the execution by fire of a captive enemy ruler named Croesus, Cyrus felt strangely humbled before the immensity of forces beyond his control. He felt himself opened up to his captive and his plight, and he spared his prisoner's life.

Herodotus gives us Cyrus's inner thoughts as he orders King Croesus released. The historian writes, "His mind was changed; he recognized that he too was a man and that it was another man, no whit less in great fortune than himself, whom he was giving alive to the fire; besides, he was afraid of what he must pay in retribution and thought again how nothing of all that is in the world of men could be secure."[3]

shalom: the Hebrew word for "peace," "well-being," and "harmony."

As one feels one's ego shrink before the otherness of God, one opens up to others—to their humanity, their gifts, and their needs. One is drawn into a shared, harmonious mutuality with neighbors, strangers, and even enemies. Like Cyrus and Croesus, one experiences a taste of *shalom* ("harmony")—a taste of the *salvation* of God.

Reverence and Community

The expressions of awe in 2 Isaiah could never have reached the sublime heights that they do without the power of a group culture behind the book. We must think of an entire community—an Isaiah "school"—as the authors of our poems.

I mentioned already other scholars' assertions that 2 Isaiah is the work of an anonymous exilic genius, a single prophet, acting alone. Yet experience has taught us that the embers of reverence soon give up their glow unless banked together with other live coals. Fellowship with others of like feeling and behavior is crucial in supporting reverence. We know this from our experiences both within the church and within modern culture.

Corporate worship is short-circuited if few in the pews feel awe. If a congregation is not singing the church's hymns with power and conviction, we feel self-conscious if we try to go it alone. Amid empty rituals, we begin suspecting that we are wasting our energy with our prayers. At times, we may feel overcome by frustration.

By the same token, daily life cannot be reverent if surrounded by self-centeredness and arrogance. In such surroundings, nobody feels like helping out others or being inspired to virtuous living. Instead, we roll our eyes, throw up our hands, and curse each other out. We lapse into a chilly utilitarianism: people get treated like numbers and nature like a commodity.

Nurturing reverence requires the help of others in articulating and expressing awe. It requires the reinforcement of hushed silences, knowing eye-contacts, and open minds. If you seek after reverence, you naturally unite with others who can share with you in a culture that embodies the virtue. Surely now it is clear that the prophetic poems of 2 Isaiah must have arisen out of a group-culture of reverence. They must have had their origins amid a communal experience that was strongly in touch with the otherness of God.

IDENTIFYING THE AUTHORS OF 2 ISAIAH

The support group behind the poems of 2 Isaiah lets slip its presence at certain key points. At Isaiah 53:1, for example, the group's prophecy has built to a climax of utter surprise. Who would have thought God's salvation would be as alien as this? What our authors now must proclaim has so unnerved them that they speak directly to us in their own voice. "Who would believe what *we* have heard?" they blurt out (NAB, emphasis added).

Other points where the writers reveal their numbers include Isaiah 62:6–7 and 66:5. Isaiah 62:6–7 speaks of sentinels posted on Zion's walls. As elsewhere in the Bible, this metaphor refers to prophetic "lookouts" who keep watch for the revelations of God. Here, they are none other than the community of 2 Isaiah, appointed to keep rounds that include prayer, proclamation, and intercession. Isaiah 66:5 is an assurance of God to this same community. Here, they are called those who "tremble."

Talk of "tremblers" refers to those who are familiar—viscerally familiar—with the awe of God. To know the Holy is to know what it means to tremble, to know soul-shaking dread. Their message is the dawning of the sacred before earth's nations. God is on the move, they believe, to "manifest His Presence" (NJPS). Their opponents, disbelieving, taunt them for their reverence.

Can we say more about the community of 2 Isaiah? Perhaps we can, if we consider that a key tool in keeping reverence alive is often ceremonial ritual. When entered into with feeling, spiritual rites form a window into God's otherness. They provide a language of reverence, which helps participants imagine an otherwise hard-to-articulate awe. Further, liturgy includes symbolic behaviors that reinforce an intuition of the Holy.

One of the great Anglican homilists of the nineteenth century, Henry Parry Liddon, recommended that when joining in corporate worship, one pray: "Lord, open mine eyes that I may see. . . . Open mine eyes that I may see thee in thy beauty, and in thy glorious presence may lose my relish for all that only belongs to time." Liddon obviously had a sense for the way liturgy should reinforce reverence.

Given the book's theology of reverence, it is not surprising to discover signs in 2 Isaiah of its authors' enthusiasm about ritual and worship. Throughout 2 Isaiah, texts such as Isaiah 44:28; 45:13; 52:1, 8; 53:10; 56:7; 60:7, 13; 62:9, 12; 64:11; and 66:6 make plain that our authors are oriented toward ceremonial purity, adherence to priestly torah, and the temple's system of sacrifices. It is easy to conclude that the community of 2 Isaiah was composed of Israelite priests.

Consider Isaiah 43:22–24. These verses show a deep care about worship offerings and sacrifices. The passage blasts Israel for neglecting God's burnt offerings (cf. Lev 1:3), sweet cane (cf. Exod 30:23), and the fat of sacrifices (cf. Lev 3:3). Israel has been too stingy even to offer the cheapest of sacrifices, the cereal offering sprinkled with incense (see NJB; cf. Lev 2:1). In redeeming Israel from exile, the Lord is going to turn all this around. Israel will be irreverent no more.

I have just mentioned that Isaiah 66:5 identifies the authors of 2 Isaiah as a group of "tremblers," quaking in awe and dread at God. The book of Ezra tells us more about the "tremblers" (see Ezra 9:4; 10:3). They appear as Ezra's supporters and colleagues in his reforms of postexilic Judah. Like him, they are oriented toward the priestly torah and the temple's sacrificial regimen. In reforming postexilic society, the group encourages separation from idolatry and making a reparation offering (Ezra 10:19; cf. Isa 53:10).

> It was the will of the LORD to crush him . . . make his life an offering for sin.
> —Isa 53:10

Apparently, 2 Isaiah's authors were in a position to direct the restored community's response to Ezra's reforming measures (Ezra 10:3). They were not simply priests. They were priests *in power* at various times after the return from exile in Babylonia.[4]

Ritual and Priestly Atonement

The startling act of reverent self-sacrifice in Isaiah 53 is 2 Isaiah's deepest mystery, and the authors sharply reveal their priestly thinking as they wrestle to interpret it. Someone has suffered and died—someone who was a servant of the Lord. Who was this anonymous Servant? What has he done? How do we respond?

Comparing the Servant to a lamb or sheep, the authors of Isaiah 53 relate his ordeal to a sacrifice at the temple (Isa 53:7). Like those sacrifices, the Servant is pure and unblemished, without fault or defect (Isa 53:9; cf. Lev 5:15, 18). Dying for other's faults, he "bore the sin" of many (Isa 53:12). To speak of "bearing sin" is to use a distinctive idiom of the priestly system of temple offerings (e.g., Lev 5:1, 17).

Israel's prophets normally call their sinful audiences to "return" or "repent" (Hebrew *shub*), but not the authors of Isaiah 53. Scouring their priestly traditions, they land on the theme that the people must "make ritual reparation" for their iniquities (Hebrew *'asham*). Specifically, they come to understand the Servant's sacrifice as the peoples' *reparation offering* (Isa 53:10), a priestly technical term (cf. Lev 5:14–6:7).

Far from randomly chosen, this unique offering fits the exiles' spiritual situation. It is the specific sacrifice one uses when in dire straits due to momentous offenses against God (Lev 5:17–19; Ezra 10:19). It is the appropriate offering if Judah's downfall was due to fatal sacrilege—irreverence before God's burning sanctity (cf. 2 Chr 36:14; Lev 5:15–16).

Still we have questions. Still we ask, "Who exactly is the Suffering Servant of 2 Isaiah?" "How can he be compared to an animal sacrifice?" Scholars have spilled jar after jar of ink puzzling over this figure, and their efforts show no sign of abating. In subsequent chapters, we too will explore the Servant's identity and work. We will find that my general theme, Isaiah's unique reverence theology, is key to elucidating the mystery.

Continuing the Conversation . . .

I heartily recommend reading the whole of 2 Isaiah for yourself in conjunction with a good commentary. One excellent learned commentary on Isaiah is *Isaiah* by Brevard S. Childs in the Old Testament Library (Louisville: Westminster John Knox, 2001). Also recommended are the notes on 2 Isaiah by Gerald T. Sheppard, "Isaiah," in *Harper's Bible Commentary,* edited by J. L. Mays (San Francisco: HarperSanFrancisco, 2000), 515–30.

For a beautifully written exposition of the virtue of reverence by an expert in classical philosophy and literature, see *Reverence: Renewing a Forgotten Virtue* by Paul Woodruff (New York: Oxford University Press, 2001).

For an introduction to the special "apocalyptic" imagination of Isaiah 56–66, see Stephen L. Cook's *The Apocalyptic Literature* in the series Interpreting Biblical Texts (Nashville: Abingdon, 2003), 111–18.

For more about the writings of the Reverence School within the Pentateuch, see the discussion of the "Priestly Torah" source in Israel Knohl's *The Sanctuary of Silence: The Priestly Torah and the Holiness School* (Minneapolis: Fortress, 1995). Note, though, that Knohl's take on the theology of this strand is very different from mine at places.

CHAPTER TWO

The Inscrutability of God in 2 Isaiah

Your God Is Too Small. In a book with this title, respected Anglican priest, author, and Bible translator J. B. Phillips tried to help his readers imagine God's true nature. He discussed many inadequate gods—that is, inadequate ways of conceiving of God. Several of these imagined deities involve a failure of reverence, including especially the god of "perennial grievance," who forever lets us down.

Sometimes, a crucial prayer fails or an undeserved tragedy strikes. Deeply disappointed, perhaps even profoundly shaken, we rail against the god of perennial grievance. Doesn't the deity care that we are blameless? Isn't God supposed to reward God's servants, not traumatize them? God is not behaving rationally. We claim grounds for complaint.

At such times, we can relate to the core complaint of 2 Isaiah's first readers. Captive in exile, the people wailed: "My way is hidden from the LORD, / And the justice due me escapes the notice of my God //" (Isa 40:27 NASB).

Although we may well empathize with such feelings and complaints, the god that they presuppose is inadequate. Such a god, who forever lets us down, is too small a deity to be viable. It is abortive—it can't "god." You know a god is too small when that deity can command no reverence, as this one surely cannot. This deity is all about us. This god's worshipers, Phillips writes, "have set up in their minds what they think God ought or ought not to do, and when he apparently fails to toe their particular line they feel a sense of grievance."[1]

> The god of "perennial grievance" is too small a deity to be viable. It is abortive—it can't "god."

We simply cannot revere that which is enslaved to our interests, a puppet-god that we manipulate through our prayers and our behavior. By definition, we can only revere that which is beyond our control and understanding. We can only revere those things truly greater than ourselves, which dwarf us and defy our ability to grasp them.

Far from worshiping a "god of perennial grievance," people of reverence confess unfamiliarity about the path of life on which they journey. Rather than claiming wisdom about what God "ought or ought not to do," they seek God's guidance on the unknown trek. God has promised to stick with them, not leave them for a minute, but

> We simply cannot revere that which is enslaved to our interests, a puppet-god that we manipulate through our prayers and our behavior.

is taking them "by a road they do not know" (Isa 42:16), a path entirely other than what they have set up in their minds. It may often make no sense to them, yet they persevere.

The Inscrutable God of 2 Isaiah

Look more closely at Isaiah 42:16, which I have just quoted. God declares, "I will lead the blind by a road they do not know"—*the blind!* Anyone can do with some friendly tips on an unknown road, but blind people are helpless in unfamiliar surroundings. In 2 Isaiah's thought, this is precisely our condition before God as mortal, finite creatures. We find ourselves helpless, in the dark, unable to control or foresee God's path for us. We push ahead only by trusting in the Lord, determining never to turn around.

For 2 Isaiah, God is beyond our control and understanding. What is more, this God is *nonrational,* at least from our human standpoint. Isaiah's view is that we humans, up against God's workings, must come to accept that we are but blind people on an unknown journey.

The inscrutability of God resists our noblest attempts to capture God, even those of creeds and systematic theologies. The formulations of religion have their purpose, but, at best, are no more than broken lights of the Holy. When we recite a creed or read a theology, we are squinting in a fog, peering through a mist. Reverence long holds its peace before attempting a lot of God-talk that says, "God is like this . . . , God is like that. . . ." It knows we cannot pin God down, cannot pin puppet strings on divine limbs. No one apprehends God, no one.

The theme of divine inscrutability in 2 Isaiah comes across most vividly perhaps in Isaiah 55:8–9. In this passage, God declares:

> [8] My thoughts are not your thoughts, /
>   nor are your ways my ways, says the LORD. //
> [9] For as the heavens are higher than the earth, /
>   so are my ways higher than your ways /
>   and my thoughts than your thoughts. //

Note the emphatic use of personal pronouns. Addressing humanity, God sets *my* thoughts over against *your* thoughts, and *my* ways over against *your* ways. The artistry emphasizes the utter impenetrability of God's plans and purposes, their foreignness to our mortal mindset. They differ not just quantitatively from our human ways, as if God's ways were simply more pure or strident than ours. No, the difference is qualitative.

Jacques Ellul, an insightful religious author, has explored our theme bravely and powerfully. If truth be told, Ellul observes, we often find that God's ways do not fit with our situation, our intelligence, and our experience. We can only find true peace, Ellul proffers, when we embrace God's radical otherness:

> When the Word of God comes to us . . . *a priori* it necessarily seems to be absurd, for it is of a different order. And our conversion does not consist in assimilating this Word so that it becomes reasonable. The absurd element persists, but from this moment what becomes absurd is the world, its wisdom, its intelligence, its power, its politics, its experience.[2]

A GOD BEYOND MORALITY?

Before we push on, I must warn you that the ramifications of our theme are profoundly unsettling, even downright jarring when we hear what comes next, that 2 Isaiah declares God's ways to transcend all workaday standards of ethics and morality. The Holy One of Israel, Isaiah asserts, takes on a guise of *amorality*! We encounter the scandal head on in Isaiah 40:14–15. Inscrutability here shades into amorality. The Lord's inscrutability radically calls into question all of our earthly notions of fair play and just desserts.

> Has the LORD ever needed anyone's advice? Does he need instruction about what is good? Did someone teach him what is right or show him the path of justice? No, for all the nations of the world are but a drop in the bucket. They are nothing more than dust on the scales. He picks up the whole earth as though it were a grain of sand. (Isa 40:14–15 NLT)

The God of these verses does not answer to human systems of justice. God appears to defy all our categories of right and wrong. 2 Isaiah pushes us to think of God with more imagination than we normally do, to permit the Holy Spirit to broaden our perspective. This poetry is demanding that we allow God a moral and ethical license inappropriate to mortals.

We experience a yawning fissure between divine holiness and practical morality.

The more we read 2 Isaiah, the more we experience a yawning fissure between divine holiness and the practical morality and fair play that we take for granted in our everyday lives. Things come to a head in Isaiah 45:7. Finally, God brazenly admits, "I create the darkness, I . . . create disaster, I, Yahweh, do all these things" (NJB). This is one of Scripture's most disturbing verses. God's admission leaves us reeling.

Plainly, the God of 2 Isaiah takes responsibility for the dark side of existence. We are left aghast, repulsed! How can we worship this deity of Isaiah's? If God creates darkness, does not worshiping God put us in danger of siding with darkness ourselves?

I create the darkness, I . . . create disaster, I, Yahweh, do all these things. —Isa 45:7 NJB

No, we will find, worshiping the God of Isaiah does not make us evil. To the contrary, it actually enjoins moral behavior upon us. For, paradoxically, as we come to discover God's radical otherness, our souls are drawn more fully to God, making us better, more other-centered persons. Discovering God as God truly is, we feel increasing awe before the towering, nonrational dimensions of the divine. More and more, we recognize our profanity and alienation from ultimate reality. The experience provokes powerful feelings of culpability and awakens a ravenous hunger for purity and virtue. We find ourselves impelled to become freer, nobler, and more selfless.

> Discovering God's radical otherness draws our souls more fully to God and makes us better, more other-centered persons.

A Solution to God's Unfairness

We are about to get some answers to our questions about God's unfairness, some remedies to our grievances against heaven. Our balm turns out to be nothing other than God's towering otherness, which heals our searing pain at life's tragic dimensions. Something miraculous happens when we come directly before the Holy in all its otherness. Theodicy—the problem of unjust suffering and trauma in the world—loses its stranglehold on our lives. A sure conviction of God's alien fairness mounts in its place. This divine inscrutability is not a hiding place for God, a way for God to sidestep theodicy; to the contrary, God's inscrutability represents a *solution* to theodicy, a balm to relieve its pain. To receive this balm is to find oneself queerly satisfied with God, reconciled with heaven.

> **theodicy:** the problem of reconciling God's power and goodness with the existence of evil and unjust suffering in the world.

The Holy One of 2 Isaiah would not leave us wallowing in frustration and bitterness at life's injustice. Rather, God longs to grace us with an inarticulate appreciation of the value and majesty of God's workings. The Lord wills that a new God-centeredness should replace all our protests and cries of unfairness at life. God uses God's *holiness* to bring about this new spiritual centeredness within us.

How does this work? It begins as God's holiness radically reorients us, giving us a completely new take on fairness. In the presence of that which rises sheer above our comprehension we find ourselves transformed. God's otherness is so completely alien that, in its presence, our ego-selves instinctively relinquish their assumed position at the center of our existence. The world around us tears at the seams and a new universe reveals itself, in which we are standing at a position quite different from where we thought we were. With us in this position, balance and fairness are restored to our lives.

We had thought that our self, our "I," was our point of reference. Our assumption had been that we were the main protagonist in our personal life journey. We were wrong. In the presence of the Holy—the uncanny inscrutability of God—we discover that we were disoriented. Our "I," we come to learn, is not our true point of reference after all. Another center grounds us, and we willingly cede our rights to it.

In the presence of the Holy, we experience a profound new humility and unselfishness, undergoing what one might call a *de-selfing* or an *un-selfing*. The experience is liberating, freeing us to let go of our claims, desserts, and old scores. Our minds clear up to perceive a larger, more encompassing fairness and majesty in reality than we could previously apprehend. We were too busy before, preoccupied with guarding and promoting our own cause.

The justice due us in life matters terribly, but discovering the profound beauty and delight of stepping off center matters more. This is a core message of 2 Isaiah. Real bliss comes only from finding life's center outside of one's self—*decentering*. The way to get there is to bask in the awful majesty of the Holy.

> *Real bliss comes only from finding life's center outside of one's self—decentering. The way to get there is to bask in the awful majesty of the Holy.*

Encountering Isaiah's Holy One opens wide our eyes of faith. We glimpse fairness from God's true, alien perspective. Far from feeling defeated, demoted, or bullied, we find ourselves enlightened, restored, and empowered. Our souls are wondrously stilled, not grievously stifled. Let me offer at least one example.

In his classic study of God's otherness, *The Idea of the Holy,* the famed theologian Rudolf Otto summarizes a short story about the tragic collapse of a mighty bridge. The narrator relates how a raging cyclone destroyed in minutes what architectural genius and back-breaking toil had taken a seeming eternity to build. He records his visit to the disaster scene, where untamed, feral nature had demolished a profound, hard-won achievement. Curiously, against all logical expectations, the scene inspires reverence, not despair.

The visitors view the sky's peculiar brightness and the ghastly majesty of the watery abyss that has swallowed the bridge. The dark estuary of the Ennobucht lies below them as a gaping, watery grave, but they sense a spirit brooding over the aqueous chaos. Indeed, they feel the tangible presence of the Lord of life and death. Overcome with wonder, they kneel.

Somehow, they have come to appreciate a mysterious value in the awesome exercise of powers that do not conform to human wishes and have dwarfed a proud human achievement. In their new, profound humility before that which utterly transcends their comprehension, their souls have found a strange new peace and energy.

An intelligible understanding of God's ways remains barred to the bridge's visitors, but they discover nonetheless that God's dealings are justified. Their souls intuitively sense the wonder of God's otherness, and repose in the mystery. Otto accounts for this as follows:

> Why did they kneel? Why did they feel constrained to do so? One does not kneel before a cyclone or the blind forces of nature, nor even before Omnipotence merely as such. But one does kneel before the wholly uncomprehended Mystery, revealed yet unrevealed, and one's soul is stilled by feeling the way of its working.[3]

Inscrutability and the Reverence School

For many religious believers, both ancient and modern, spirituality is a rather *practical* thing. These believers worship and obey God, and trust that God, in turn, will faithfully look out for them. In this, they are not necessarily selfish. Beyond individual concerns, they pray for a just, stable society, for their community and nation. They come to church, or the courtyard of the ancient temple, with supplications for fine weather, or victory in war, or wisdom for their leaders.

This practical spirituality appears so natural that it is surprising to discover its foreignness to the Reverence School. We search the Scriptures of the school in vain for prayer requests in Zion's sacred courtyards. We come up empty looking for temple rites supporting bountiful harvests or the kingdom's political health. The priests receive no guidance in the Reverence School strand for drawing the Lord down into any of the dynamics of workaday life.

How can the Reverence School take this approach? It all has to do with the peculiar workings of reverence on the human soul, the transforming effect on people of the awesome majesty of the Holy.

When faced with the Holy, people quickly become radically un-self-interested, forgetting about their burning drive to satisfy their own needs and desires.

According to the Reverence School, the temple is not a place for drawing God down to earth but for inarticulate awe at God's loftiness. It is where the soul approaches the inscrutable God, is drawn upward, and is overcome. God's mystery rises sheer above the worshiper in the temple's courts, towering to heights of which we know nothing and which can have no meaning for us. God abides above the temple's sacral courts, "Speechlessly, without beginning, Sun that never rose! Vast, adorable, and winning, Day that hath no close!"[4]

The temple is not a place for drawing God down to earth but for inarticulate awe at God's loftiness. It is where the soul approaches the inscrutable God, is drawn upward, and is overcome.

Fascinatingly, the Reverence School has little interest in what other parts of the Bible refer to as the "covenant" enacted between God and Israel on Mount Sinai. It knows of no covenantal rewards and punishments. Instead, the school's texts describe God giving Israel a *testimony* on Mount Sinai (Exod 25:16, 21 NJB and NIV). Israel is to obey the God-given *testimony* with no thought of recompense, no thought of rewards for their loyalty. The people are to follow God's commands simply because God desires it, not because of any two-way agreement or any guarantee that God will meet their needs.

The form of the *testimony* given on Mount Sinai after the exodus presupposes the dynamic effects of awe on human beings. Overcome by awareness of God's sublime dimensions, our daily concerns become surprisingly trivial. They are overshadowed by a consuming desire to embrace God's wondrousness and to place our everyday, ordinary lives before God as an offering.

The provocative Israeli biblical scholar Israel Knohl has hit the nail on the head in describing Israel's *testimony* from God:

> With the revelation of [the sublime, *numinous*] aspect of the divinity—which cannot be described through any anthropomorphizing imagery, and which transcends reason and morality and is independent of the relation of reward and punishment—humans recognize their true status and are transformed into people who "worship through love," without expecting any recompense for their deeds.[5]

THE HARDENING OF PHARAOH'S HEART

In the theology of the Reverence School, God reveals God's self on earth not to legislate justice and stability but to inspire awe and feelings of reverence. Leviticus 10:3 (RS) sums up God's purposes: "By those who come near me I will be treated as holy, And before all the people I will be honored" (NASB). To accomplish this, God leans on the inscrutable, amoral nature of divinity, as comes across most emphatically in God's intervention at the exodus, particularly in God's manipulation of Pharaoh's mind and will.

According to Exodus 9:12 (RS), "The LORD hardened the heart of Pharaoh" so that he kept Israel enslaved despite an ongoing plague of boils. Intervening directly in Moses and Aaron's attempt to win their people's freedom, God effectively assured Pharaoh's obstinacy. In doing so, God actively promoted darkness and chaos.

God's manipulation of Pharaoh significantly worsened the Israelites' situation. It prolonged their experience of persecution in Egypt and further aggravated their enslavers. With Egypt's ruler now immovably obdurate, the Hebrew people had no prospect of a quick and ready escape from their enslavement.

Without a doubt, the Lord's priority was not freeing Israel, despite their suffering. Rather, God acted primarily to evoke dismay and dread of the Holy on earth. Stating this directly, God declared, "I will harden the hearts of the Egyptians . . . and I will be honored through Pharaoh and all his army, through his chariots and his horsemen" (Exod 14:17 NASB). To "be honored" (Hebrew *nikbad*) means to be regarded with peculiar dread, to have the world react to you with the specific emotions associated with eerie transcendent *otherness* (*viz.* the *numinous*).

> **the numinous:** that which conveys an uncanny sense of preternatural otherness, of the sublime, holy, and transcendent.

Delaying the exodus, hardening Pharaoh's heart, God took the opportunity to establish divine otherness publicly and incontestably. God used the occasion to "out" Egypt's idols of security and control for what they were—nothing more than puppet-gods, abortively diminutive. This demonstrated for all to see that the Lord's purported rivals, both human and "divine," were pure embarrassments.

Do not misunderstand. The God of Israel is no petty deity, preoccupied with the divine self and aloof from our brokenness. God is assuredly concerned with our individual lots, but emphasizes public knowledge of the Holy because it is crucial to human redemption. Other orientations, which reduce the gospel to something banal and practical, lack true saving power.

What do I mean by this? What is the matter with purely *practical* spiritualities? To worship "practical" puppet-gods, such as the god of perennial grievance, is to focus on our own security, comfort, and ability to manipulate the world. It is to abandon the desire for the wondrous, and labor instead at propping up our own autonomy. It is only as persons discover and enlarge the virtue of reverence, getting to know the one God who is not "too small," that hope is rekindled. As they meet God in God's dreadfulness and otherness, people let go of all their pretensions of control that have kept life cold and brutish. Leaving behind their pains to manipulate the world, which have been damning them, they turn in self-renunciation to God.

> As they meet God in God's dreadfulness and otherness, people let go of all their pretensions of control that have kept life cold and brutish.

In embracing the Holy One—the numinous God, who is simultaneously dreadful and blissful—human beings find that God has brought out the best in them. Abandoning everything to God, they find that God easily surpasses their wildest dreams and satisfies their cries for justice. Now that's salvation—in fact, that's ecstasy.

A Conversation with Isaiah 45:4–8

The Reverence School's emphasis that God is beyond our minds' grasp, beyond our notions of fair play, blossoms in 2 Isaiah. This becomes obvious in several central poems. Let us examine parts of two of them together, starting with Isaiah 45:4–8.

This passage is part of a larger prophecy about the Lord's mysterious use of King Cyrus of Persia in liberating Judah's exiles from Babylonian captivity. The text is included in our Episcopal Sunday Lectionary, and is an excellent entrée into the sheer tremendousness of God in 2 Isaiah.

> lectionary: a tabulation of scriptural passages to be read in services of the church. Most Sunday lectionaries repeat on a three-year cycle.

Verses 4–8 continue some direct words of the Lord to Cyrus, God's anointed instrument. (Although Cyrus is the ostensive addressee, the prophecy aims first to encourage the Judean exiles.) The "I" who is speaking is God; the "you" is Cyrus.

⁴ For the sake of my servant Jacob, /
  and Israel my chosen, //
I call you by your name, /
  I surname you, though you do not know me. //
⁵ I am the LORD, and there is no other; /
  besides me there is no god. /
  I arm you, though you do not know me, //
⁶ so that they may know, from the rising of the sun /
  and from the west, that there is no one besides me; /
  I am the LORD, and there is no other. //
⁷ I form light and create darkness, /
  I make weal and create woe; /
  I the LORD do all these things. //

⁸ Shower, O heavens, from above, /
  and let the skies rain down righteousness; //
let the earth open, that salvation may spring up, /
  and let it cause righteousness to sprout up also; /
  I the LORD have created it. //

The poem presents a scandalous God. This God is out to disorient people, defy their logic, and make their knees shake (v. 7). This is a deity who creates darkness, who is responsible for chaos and woe.

Shockingly, the Lord is getting a foreign ruler, Cyrus, involved in Israel's restoration. This heathen king was now to become the "anointed" of the Lord (v. 1), called into service by God "for the sake of Israel my chosen" (v. 4). He is to be armed by God for battle (v. 5).

The verb "know" appears several times in our short poem. God is at work with a purpose: to make *known* God's mystery. The effort starts now, with this poem, with Cyrus himself. The Persian ruler thus far has been ignorant of the Lord's sponsorship, but that is about to change. It certainly changed for Pharaoh at the time of the exodus from Egypt. Earth experienced the sheer, amoral dynamism of the Holy then, and is about to do so again. God is bringing about a new exodus, bringing the Judean exiles out of Babylonia just as God delivered the children of Israel out of Egypt.

Pharaoh, at the first exodus, demanded that Moses and Aaron prove themselves by showing him a sign (Exod 7:9 RS). He doubtless expected a sleight of hand at best. Skeptical and arrogant, he was ill-prepared to experience a "wonder" of God, a gesture of dazzling, inscrutable power. To his shock, instead of performing a cheap parlor trick, Aaron throws down his staff and it becomes a hideous monster (Hebrew *tannin*). Before he could blink, Pharaoh was face to face with a slithering chaos dragon (Exod 7:10 RS).[6] With this wonder, God struck a dissonant chord and the earth shivered. Hairs stood up on the backs of necks. Sometimes, as here, the world experiences God's holy power as darkness and terror—disorder and destabilization. As God says, "I . . . create darkness, I . . . create woe."

It is now seven hundred years later, and God is no longer addressing Pharaoh but Cyrus the Great. As God addresses the Persian king, God explains a mystery of which Cyrus is not yet aware. God is at work in his march against Babylonia, and the purpose is not merely to snatch Israel out of exile. God is at work, as at the first exodus, to make divine wondrousness known in the world, to display it out in the open.

Pharaoh learned of God's awesome power to his dismay, but King Cyrus will learn astonishment at God in a different manner. His coming conquest of Babylon is part of an infinitely grand divine strategy. Instead of meeting up with a chaos dragon, he will find all barriers kicked down ahead of him, and his road cleared and paved. The effect will be just as eerie, just as inscrutable. God has found a new way to throw earth off balance, to strike a dissonant chord. God is rolling out a red carpet for a heathen king!

Cyrus's imminent success had better humble him. It will all be due to his undeserved role in a grand plan of God to bless the world (see v. 8). God has access to his mind and controls his paths, just as with the Pharaoh of the exodus. When Cyrus sees Zion restored and the earth bloom salvation (v. 8), he will realize this. He will learn that the Lord, the God of Israel, has guided and inspired him and given him his victories.

King Cyrus will come to know God's wondrousness and so will all the nations of the world. Verse 6, the climax of our poem, drives this home. It reveals the central purpose behind God's unforeseen and unimagined commissioning of Cyrus. This purpose is that people the world over will know God in God's full uniqueness and eerie otherness. God wants universal reverence.

No one will be able to miss the sheer wonder of God shining through the spectacle of Cyrus. Foreign heathens are not Jewish messiahs! This is sheer scandal; it is dazzling and inscrutable. This pagan is about to defeat Israel's enemies, free the Judeans from exile, and rebuild Zion and its temple. His lightning progress in doing all this will be nothing short of astounding, the wondrous power of God displayed on the world stage.

God wants everyone, from east to west, to focus on God, and on God alone. The number of times God uses the pronoun "I" in our poem is remarkable. In four short verses, "I" appears six times. Six times more God speaks of "me" or "my." Moreover, the poem repeats the full statement "I am Yahweh [the LORD]" three times. It appears in the proclamation "I am the LORD, and there is no other" (v. 5 and v. 6) and again at the conclusion of v. 7, "I am the LORD" (NASB).

In all this "I" talk the God of 2 Isaiah is being neither vain nor egotistical. It has nothing to do with divine narcissism. God's rhetoric is uttered with the purpose of blessing the world, for the sake of transforming life so that salvation springs up from the ground (v. 8).

This is the same rhetoric that characterizes the texts of the Reverence School about the exodus (see Exod 6:2, 6; 7:5 RS).[7] God wants us to grasp the divine statement "I am Yahweh" in its essence. To do so is to shrink back like Pharaoh's magicians, exclaiming, "This is the finger of God!" (Exod 8:19 RS). It is to abandon all pretensions of control, putting aside all puppet-gods and parlor tricks.

> The magicians said to Pharaoh, "This is the finger of God!" —Exod 8:19

As we saw emphasized in the Reverence School, the worship of puppet-gods, too small for reverence, is what is condemning the world, frustrating God's desire to bless it. Such gods cannot keep the embers of reverence aglow in our lives. Made in our image, they keep us focused on ourselves, condemning us to arrogance, oppression, and loneliness.

What we need desperately is to know the God of 2 Isaiah, who declares, "Besides me there is no god" (v. 5), "There is no one besides me" (v. 6). Before this God, who is incomparable, thus beyond all mental apprehension, we become conscious of our human limitations and mutual interdependence. We abandon our self-focus, just as the Reverence School taught, and turn outward to God and our frail, human neighbors.

We become human—fully human. Only then will right living with right choices (Hebrew *tsedaqah*) sprout up on earth (v. 8). The joy that verse 8 exudes at the prospect of such a sprouting righteousness is palpable. Its two poetic lines form a short "Snoopy dance," a hymnic interlude celebrating God's coming wonders.

Let me sum up. Our poem is all about the virtue of reverence and its ultimate expression: abandoning ourselves to God. It is toward this end that its lines emphasize knowing God in all God's eerie singularity. It is with the goal of universal right living with right choices in mind (Hebrew *tsedaqah*) that God in our poem hammers home "I am the LORD."

A Conversation with Isaiah 45:9–13

Immediately after the little "Snoopy dance" in Isaiah 45:8 a new poem begins, taking the message of 2 Isaiah in a somewhat different direction. The theme remains the inscrutable character of God, but now Israel and the nations, not Cyrus, are the conversation partners. The poem is for all people, both outside Israel and within it, who are in pain over the world events around them. It is for all of us who are trying to cope with what often appears to be an unbearably unbalanced and senseless world. Isaiah 45:9–13 reads as follows:

> 9 Woe to you who strive with your Maker, /
>   earthen vessels with the potter! //
> Does the clay say to the one who fashions it, "What are you making"? /
>   or "Your work has no handles"? //
> 10 Woe to anyone who says to a father, "What are you begetting?" /
>   or to a woman, "With what are you in labor?" //
>
> 11 Thus says the LORD, /
>   the Holy One of Israel, and its Maker: //
> Will you question me about my children, /
>   or command me concerning the work of my hands? //

¹² I made the earth, /
    and created humankind upon it; //
it was my hands that stretched out the heavens, /
    and I commanded all their host. //
¹³ I have aroused Cyrus in righteousness, /
    and I will make all his paths straight; //
he shall build my city /
    and set my exiles free, //
not for price or reward, /
    says the LORD of hosts. //

The rise of Cyrus and his endorsement by God threatened the exiles' faith. It left them dazed, sapped, and sleepless. If there was to be a new exodus, they imagined a new Moses would lead it, an exemplary Israelite who knew the Lord, Yahweh. Cyrus did not fit the bill. He was not even Semitic, never mind Jewish. He neither knew the Lord nor understood the significance of God's people, Israel. Yet here was God, insisting, "I have aroused Cyrus in righteousness, / and I will make all his paths straight; // he shall build my city / and set my exiles free //" (v. 13).

This was tough news, too tough to swallow. You can imagine the exiles' reaction: "This can't be happening. We deserve a *real* liberation, a *real* Moses with a shepherd's staff and two tablets of stone! Where is the God of justice?"

The poem addresses the exiles' pain—their struggle with darkness and *theodicy*. Theodicy is a huge challenge to faith, the eventual flash point of almost any meaningful conversation about God. It threatens our cherished ideas of truth and justice, and, at times, shatters them to smithereens. It exposes key roads we thought led to God as mere blind alleys.

Look closely at verses 9–10, and imagine the grievances the exiles must be voicing. You can hear their anguish in their words: "O God, what were you thinking? Are you an imbecile? Your work shows no skill! How clumsy can you get?" (v. 9; I am paraphrasing).

This is the language of grieving people, doing the only thing that makes them feel better. They are lashing out. C. S. Lewis railed at God in similar language when cancer took the life of his wife, Joy

Davidman Gresham. In his grief, he imagined God as a "Cosmic Sadist," baiting and trapping us like feral cats. Our poem is a dialogue with Judah's despondent exiles and with later believers, such as C. S. Lewis, who are at a similar place of intense grief. It paraphrases what they are thinking. Then, using the power of poetry, it evokes awe and reverence in order to heal them.

The metaphor of a potter shaping a lump of clay is especially powerful and healing. God *is* manipulating and shaping the course of history, our poem asserts, but as a potter, not a sadist. Where God is taking us is out of our control, but is not sadistic or spiteful simply because it involves pain. A potter needs to work the unformed clay, and that twists and bends us. We have pain because, as clay, we are still an unformed mass, not yet the unique new creation the potter has in mind (v. 9).

Verse 10 gives us a related metaphor from the sphere of human reproduction. As an embryo, we humbly receive our biological identity as a gift. Although untold transformations lie ahead of us as we develop in the womb, it is not for us to object. Neither do we have any say over the coming trauma at our birthing, although it is obviously in our best interests to endure the process of delivery into the world.

Inconsolable and struggling with his faith, C. S. Lewis found his reflections moving in this very direction. He found himself forced to reckon with a transcendent, awe-inspiring God who has the world on a potter's wheel. Before God's towering holiness, we mortals are but lumpy clay. Lewis writes:

> Is it rational to believe in ... the Cosmic Sadist, the spiteful imbecile? I think it is, if nothing else, too anthropomorphic. .... [A more suitable picture] preserves mystery. Therefore room for hope. Therefore room for a dread or awe.[8]

Our poem rings with the concepts of dread and awe that Lewis mentions. These are the concepts with the power to help us find peace with the world's darkness and dissonance. Verse 11 explicitly identifies the Lord as "the Holy One of Israel, and its Maker." The title identifies Israel's God as the supreme embodiment of the numinous, that which is disturbingly other than the mundane world.

Verse 12 speaks of the divine wonder manifest in the cosmos' creation. Its poetry uses emphatic first-person pronouns to insist that this wonder pertains to the Lord alone: "*I, I* made the earth . . . *I,* with *my own* hands, stretched out the heavens" (my translation).

AESTHETICS AND THEODICY

In our poem, the Lord is a potter. As such, our God is an artist, a God of *aesthetics.* Consider the ramifications. A potter—an artist— is focused foremost on beauty, not ethics, intelligibility, and rationality. If God is fundamentally an artist, we must quickly come to grips with it. It may help us deal with our pain at the lack of stability and safety in God's world.

aesthetics: that which concerns beauty, both its nature and its expression.

If God is a potter, God's pots and jars consist of God's good creation: "the earth" and "humankind upon it," "the heavens," and "all their host" (v. 12). As artwork, creation and all its components take on a new character for us. They no longer need to be all logic and decency, completely lean and prim. Indeed, they cannot be these things if, as successful art, they are to have the power to grip and inspire us, to fill us with conviction and commitment.

An artist derives satisfaction and delight from the free, sometimes extravagant, exercise of creativity. We do not complain if she fashions a gallery piece with no handles, since we know that practicality and consumer safety are not her concerns. Artwork aims at conveying truth and wonder. Usefulness and propriety are not its priorities.

The workings of art are like the workings of love. Falling in love is nonrational, messy, and erotic. A lover's quality of being is what enthralls us, not intelligible features that we can articulate. It does not matter that the person cannot do math or pokes fun at our favorite jacket. "Imperfections" such as these only magnify our love. Lovesick, we drop everything, and focus on seeking the other. Such lovesickness mirrors, in some small degree, an ideal relationship with God.

Rudolf Otto rightly spoke of the ability of the sublime to still our anguish at the world's cruel imperfections and injustices, to relax our souls and grant us full contentment. Like an exquisite lover, the Holy mocks at all conceiving, but fascinates, overfills, and overwhelms the heart. Its sheer, overabounding value appeases and satisfies us, although, like love, it is eminently impractical and extravagant, even nonrational.

Beyond being impractical and nonrational, great works of art may be feral and unnerving. They may include dissonance—grating, unstable, even chaotic elements alongside soothing ones. The impression of tension or clash can captivate and convict. It is often central to art's energy, persuasiveness, and aura of truth.

Consider the wonder of true beauty and you will realize that it is fundamentally *persuasive.* Beauty has the capacity to fill us with a certitude, the sort of certitude for which we are willing to wrestle and struggle, to invest much, to risk a great deal. Without its wildness and dissonance, beauty would not have this effect on us. It would not ring true, would not convince us. It would not get our hearts pumping as it does; it would not get our adrenaline flowing.

Consider how a beautiful lover affects us. Such a lover provokes us and overturns our fixed conceptions. Lovers who never surprise us, challenge us, or transform us do not excite us. An ideal lover must be soundly independent, real, and *other.* He or she must resist, allude, and stretch us. Experiencing him or her ever anew keeps us alert, present, and alive. The person's beauty actually delivers us, saves us from our self-concern.

For God to be God, worthy of reverence, our cherished ideas of the divine must constantly be exposed as inaccurate. Our imaginative construals of God and of God's workings on earth must forever be overturned and shattered. This necessarily requires a universe with inherent dissonance and eerie chaos. Reality can take no other form. In the language of our poem, we must come to see that our need for every clay pot to have a handle is limiting and immature.

The sublime not only convicts and persuades us but also captivates and enslaves us. The beholder, overcome by the sublime, determines to become its bond-person, to support and serve it. Such service is for beauty's sake alone; it is gratuitous, purely un-self-interested, unrecompensed. We serve the cause of beauty without ulterior motives, without desiring to become beautiful ourselves, without even needing a guarantee that we will benefit from beauty in any way.

Confirming this truth about the nature of the sublime, King Cyrus, our poem asserts, must act without payment. He must serve God *gratis*. His carrying out of God's mission is explicitly "not for price or reward" (v. 13). God has neither struck a deal with Cyrus nor made him any promises. Cyrus must do the divine bidding out of sheer respect for who God is, out of sheer awe at the sublime beauty of God and God's purposes.

Continuing the Conversation . . .

The classic treatment of the nonrational, numinous side of God is Rudolf Otto's *The Idea of the Holy*, translated by J. W. Harvey (London: Oxford University Press, 1923). For some exciting insights into the relationship of fairness and our experience of the sublime, read Elaine Scarry, *On Beauty and Being Just* (Princeton: Princeton University Press, 1999).

For a spiritual masterpiece about the emergence of a renovated faith amid dissonance and grief, read C. S. Lewis, *A Grief Observed* (New York: Bantam Books, 1976).

I hope that now as we have begun digging into 2 Isaiah's depths, you are becoming more interested in finding good commentaries on these Scriptures. There are many excellent commentaries on 2 Isaiah beyond the works of B. S. Childs and G. T. Sheppard, which I have already mentioned. For a classic liberal commentary, highly attuned to 2 Isaiah's form and rhetorical beauty, see James Muilenburg's "The Book of Isaiah, Chapters 40–66: Introduction and Exegesis" in volume 5 of *The Interpreter's Bible*, edited by G. A. Buttrick (Nashville: Abingdon, 1956), 381–773. For a detailed evangelical commentary, with rich theological insights, see John N. Oswalt, *The Book of Isaiah: Chapters 40–66* (Grand Rapids: Eerdmans, 1998). For a careful new translation and up-to-date historical commentary, see Joseph Blenkinsopp, *Isaiah 40–55: A New Translation with Introduction and Commentary*, volume 19A of the Anchor Bible (New York: Doubleday, 2000).

CHAPTER THREE

Reverence and the Collapse of Pride and Ignorance

Near the end of his fantastic journey, the character John in C. S. Lewis's story *The Pilgrim's Regress* passes the homes of two horrid figures, Superbia and Ignorantia. They are daughters of the Enemy, the dark, burning rival of God. Together, the two sisters symbolize much of what entraps humankind, keeping us from peace, harmony, and joy.

First, John encounters Superbia, whose name means *pride.* All her life, she has striven for mastery of her surroundings and control of her body. She has slavishly cleansed the plateau on which she lives, removing every speck of dust, moss, and fungus. Just as obsessively, she has starved and mutilated herself into something completely clean and icy. A living skeleton, she has paid a dear price for sloughing off all that is "common or unclean," for achieving the transcendence that she claims for herself.

Superbia claims to have achieved the supernatural. She boasts of an unstained soul, of all iniquities blotted out. She describes herself as a pure, bright mineral, of having made herself into a "mortal God." "Myself am to myself, a mortal God," she sings, "a self-contained Unwindowed monad, unindebted and unstained."[1]

As John and his party pass by, Superbia is croaking a song, broadcasting her distorted self-understanding. She has scrubbed her plateau clean of all profaneness, starved her body completely pure. She has "scoured [her] rock clean from the filthy earth," made her soul "hard, pure, bright."

The unblemished, shimmering power of the Holy is understandably attractive to Superbia. In sheer irreverence, however, she has striven to control and manipulate that for which she longs. Sadly, her Lilliputian efforts are deluded and futile. If she was ever to experience the Holy for real, she would utterly despair.

"Self-contained" and "Unwindowed," Superbia can have no real encounter with that which is greater than she is, beyond all familiarity. In her disgust for what is soft and moist, she has foolishly renounced her vulnerability and finitude, preempting any experience of awe. She has effectively isolated herself from the only thing that could save her from her misery.

All human beings wrestle with pride, though few of us go to the extremes of Superbia. Repeatedly, we obsess on the trite and finite, squelching every beckoning to our souls from beyond our mean plateau. We grasp at temporal objects to satisfy immortal longings. We use banal techniques to attempt a spiritual ascent, yet our lungs strain to inflate our balloon of pretensions. We become lonely and lean atop our self-made pedestal.

The Bible is well familiar with the spirit of Superbia. Perhaps most compellingly, she appears within Scripture in the guise of conjurers, magicians, and idol makers. These religious professionals share a common obsession with making divinity manageable, sizing it down in scale and proportion. They claim the wherewithal to manipulate the Holy. They devote their lives to the effort, striving to snag what is *other* by the tail. Such experts claim mastery over mystery, unmindful of how far they are out on a limb. Like Superbia, they are fools to domesticate the Holy. They are deluded in supposing that the wild, beastly qualities of creation might be manageable. No mere mortal can wrangle successfully with the world's feral and lethal dimensions. No one dares harness earth's dragons of chaos. Dread swirls around their teeth; dismay dances before them.

The poetry of 2 Isaiah captures the dread and dismay that adheres to the cosmos. It rightly insists we own up to our frailty. No mortal can steady what God keeps off balance, subdue a creation that God has made free. Superbia's efforts to cleanse and control her world are resoundingly vain.

The Critique of Idolatry in 2 Isaiah

Superbia is the sworn enemy of 2 Isaiah. To our authors' way of thinking, her spirit represents all that is wrong with the world. As long as pride and ignorance reign, the lifestyle of reverence has no room to take root. 2 Isaiah has no choice but to engage this foe, and the weapon of choice is surprising: it is merciless satire.

Within 2 Isaiah, satirical poetry decries all who dare harness divinity, especially the manufacturers and users of idols (see Isa 40:18–20; 41:6–7; 44:9–20; 46:1–7). Idolatry was especially well developed in Babylonia, and many exiles doubtless joined in its practice. That is probably why it is specially targeted

> **satire:** use of the language of wit, irony, and sarcasm to expose and ridicule vices and follies.

Worship images for 2 Isaiah are prideful tools for putting reins on the numinous. Their visual nature makes heaven something manageable, something proportional to human reality. They lead us to think we can lay hold of divinity, grasp it, and use it to prop up our lives. When idolatry spreads, self-sufficiency triumphs. This gives a quick victory to Superbia's spirit.

But idolatry is fundamentally wrongheaded. It must be stopped. The Holy dwells in freedom, apart from our human plateau, unchained to any image. If idolatry could overcome this freedom, tether down the divine, then the elements of our surroundings could become good as gods. As dark lords, they would hold us in service.

> *The Holy dwells in freedom, apart from our human plateau, unchained to any image.*

There is continuity, idolaters believe, between an idol and the god that it offers up to us. The god's power is immanent in it, tangible, present, and available. Immanent within the worship image, flowing out to the beholder, spiritual energy seems within human grasp, available to us as a shield and a tool. Succumbing to the temptation to access this power of idols is pride.

2 Isaiah's poems mock the idea that idols can channel us power. Should one pay for the best god that money can buy? The idea seems fantastic, but these poems assure us that rich idolaters do not hesitate to "lavish gold from the purse, and weigh out silver in the scales— they hire a goldsmith, who makes it into a god; then they fall down and worship!" (Isa 46:6). Reading such satire, it is hard not to chuckle.

Ordinary people produce idols, our poems insist, using common, everyday materials. They make them of their own device, out of their own imaginations. To gaze at their work yields no vision of *otherness*. Where is the awe in a fancy commodity, a piece of merchandise?

One might object to Isaiah's language as mean and intolerant. Isn't this a rather narrow line of thought? After all, we *do* hold some art worthy of awe, such as the *Venus de Milo*. Can we not simply appreciate ancient Babylonian idols in the same way? Why not consider them masterworks? Perhaps some really do find their beauty or strangeness empowering.

Some products of human culture and religion do indeed inspire reverence, but certain conditions must apply. Technically speaking, an object of reverence must be something we no longer fully understand or something we cannot change without destroying. If we can apprehend something, control it, or channel its power, then reverence, by definition, is out of place.[2]

More to the point, although we sometimes justifiably revere artworks, it would be ridiculous to worship them. They are not deities, worthy of veneration and service. Ancient Near Easterners did serve idols, succumbing to the same delusions as Superbia. They anointed them, kissed them, prayed to them, and generally treated them as divine. They also sweated for them.

THE SWEATY LABOR OF IDOLATRY

People not only worship idols, according to 2 Isaiah, but also exert great efforts on their behalf. Consider the frenetic service described in Isaiah 46:6–7: "they hire a goldsmith"; "they fall down and worship"; "they lift it to their shoulders"; "they carry it"; "they set it in its place." The poetry is all about human labor on behalf of idols. The people are the subject of the six Hebrew verbs. Their idol is the syntactical object, passively receiving the action.

Idol worshipers are really sweating, doing heavy work. Yet we should not be too quick to judge them. During Advent, don't we act just the same? In the season before Christmas, our frenzied shopping has us running around and out of breath. We bear the heavy burden of creating a holy experience for ourselves and our families. It is a lot of work satisfying our family's immortal longings. Achieving high spirituality takes a lot of scrabbling. If only we could imagine a way of escape, a way to find rest for our souls.

In Isaiah's poetry, no one else besides the idolaters is breaking a sweat, certainly not the worship image. The idol "stands there"; "it cannot move"; "it does not answer" (Isa 46:7). Eugene H. Petersen paraphrases the irony of the situation wonderfully: "They carry [their idol] around in holy parades, then take it home and put it on a shelf. And there it sits, day in and day out, a dependable god, always right where you put it. Say anything you want to it, it never talks back. Of course, it never does anything either!" (Isa 46:7, THE MESSAGE).

The parallels with Superbia's lifestyle are striking. She craves a dependable spiritual world. To achieve it, she spends endless hours employing all means at her disposal to primp herself and polish her surroundings.

When pilgrim John first sees her, Superbia is preoccupied and frantic, creating more tumult than a mob of Christmas shoppers. "Scrabbling and puddering to and fro," she is scraping and scrubbing her bare plateau clean. Obsessed, she claims to have "scoured my rock."[3]

In effect, Superbia has made herself a slave, chained to her mop and steel wool. She has become a "famished creature." Sweat and self-deprivation have reduced her to a skeleton with "skin stretched over its bones," "eyes flaming in the sockets of its skull."

USE YOUR BRAIN!

The poems of 2 Isaiah contrast two strategies for living. One can sweat—slaving for idols—or one can think. Our poems exhort us to work at the latter, to use our God-given minds.

In 2 Isaiah, the Lord asks people to think because that is the sure path to efficacious living. Once you start thinking, nothing can stop you. It is the way to right choices and right risks, to solid ground, and harmony of mind and soul. "Remember," "consider," and "recall," Isaiah 46:8 instructs the exiles. You must think your way free from the narcosis of idols.

The Holy One of Israel is outside of the cosmos, other than the system, in a position to direct history for God's good pleasure. That is exactly what is going on. Merely recall God's mighty acts of salvation. Merely remember the power of the prophetic word to unfold the future. Then you will know that God is steering earth's history. Then you will discover that God is the hope of getting life right.

All this is obvious, apparent to human intelligence, in 2 Isaiah's view. The problem with idolaters is that they are not using their brains (Isa 44:18–19). If they were to start thinking, they would realize their deities have no guidance to offer for the long haul.

> Nor do they comprehend or understand and say to themselves: "I burned half of it in the fire—yes, I baked bread over the coals; I roasted meat and ate it. With the rest of it should I make a disgusting idol? Should I bow down to dry wood?" —Isa 44:19 NET

Continuous with the human plateau, the puppet-gods did not make the world and do not control its direction. Caught up in the world just as we are, they cannot explain the course of history or make promises for the future. How can they help us get God's wind in our sails, if they have no way of forecasting the wind's direction?

The puppet-gods make many promises, of course, but only the ignorant can possibly believe them. Enter Ignorantia ("Ignorance"), Superbia's sister. In C. S. Lewis's story, the pilgrims encounter Ignorantia some miles beyond Superbia's dwelling. They observe her long enough to gain some solid impressions. She is credulous, an easy prey for false advertisers. She puts her trust in false claims, leading to real disappointment and pain. Her specific frustrations, and those of her followers, are eerily familiar to readers today. Her partisans are all victims of commercial claims. "Their labor-saving devices multiply drudgery; . . . their amusements bore them; their rapid production of food leaves half of them starving; and their devices for saving time have banished leisure from their country."[4]

We humans are a gullible lot. We are able to convince ourselves that human diligence and innovation, in which we place our trust, can actually fulfill us. We need to get in touch with what is really going on. God is at work to bless creation and wants to bear us along to the blessing's fulfillment. Only such blessing can meet our deep, immortal longings.

A Background to Idolatry in the Reverence School

The critique of pride and idolatry in 2 Isaiah has a venerable pedigree. Already in the Scriptures of the Reverence School, God exposes the folly of Superbia and Ignorantia. Above all, this happened at the exodus from Egypt. God was at work in the exodus, proving the two sisters both gullible and complacent.

The spirit of Ignorantia was present during the exodus in all those duped by Egypt's magicians. For a time, they gulled everyone with their charms (Exod 7:11, 22; 8:2 RS). Soon enough, however, God unmasked their naïveté. Truly, the Lord is a God who "frustrates the omens of liars, and makes fools of diviners." God "turns back the wise, and makes their knowledge foolish" (Isa 44:25).

Some biblical versions of the exodus have little or nothing to say about Pharaoh's magicians, but the Reverence School strand develops their role. Its authors are aware of our addictive drive to control the Holy, to manipulate shimmering divinity. Aware of our compulsion, it confronts and overturns it.[5]

Pharaoh summons his magicians after Aaron's wonder, his transforming his staff into a dragon (Exod 7:8–13 RS). Initially, the magician's charms are persuasive. Impressively, they too turn their staffs into dragons, similar to Aaron's. Doubts immediately arise, however, about the long-term efficacy of their powers. Their secret arts lack staying power. "Aaron's staff swallowed up theirs" (Exod 7:12).

Later, the magicians are unable to duplicate the plague of gnats that Aaron summons forth (Exod 8:16–19 RS). As Aaron reaches out his staff and strikes the earth, the ground streams forth vermin. Pharaoh's magicians are unable to compete. They can neither produce gnats themselves nor get rid of Aaron's gnats.

Imagine the shudders as Egypt fills with gnats, multiplying and swarming everywhere. There are gnats gnawing at beasts, gnats biting at people. Gnats, gnats, gnats! The infestation spreads out of control, with nowhere to hide. They were "on humans and animals alike; all the dust of the earth turned into gnats" (Exod 8:17 RS). Dismay dances at the spectacle. The numinous looms large, and Egypt is undone. God has stepped forth; reality is off kilter. The magicians in particular shrink in horror. "This is the finger of God!" they quaver (Exod 8:19 RS).

It is not the gnats, however, but the plague of boils that spells the magician's definitive defeat (Exod 9:8–12 RS). Moses and Aaron fling kiln ash into the air at the Lord's command, and it blows over Egypt. Landing on both humans and animals, the soot spawns festering sores on everyone's skin. No one is spared, not even the magicians.

Stricken by the inflammation of their flesh, the magicians cannot confront Moses, never mind duplicate the plague. So much for the secret spells and magic arts of the worldly wise! To take a stand before the ineffable is inevitably to be confounded. "The magicians could not stand before Moses because of the boils, for the boils afflicted the magicians as well as all the Egyptians" (Exod 9:11 RS).

The charms and spells of magicians may sometimes manipulate nature, but they cannot connect with the isolated sovereignty of the Lord. No one can tether the Lord's mysterious will.

The charms and spells of magicians may sometimes manipulate nature, but they cannot connect with the isolated sovereignty of the Lord. No one can tether the Lord's mysterious will or channel the wondrous power of divinity. One cannot apprehend the Holy. In the end each idolater suffers dismay.

RESISTING ANTHROPOMORPHISM

A big reason idols so offend reverence thinking is that by their very nature they *anthropomorphize* (or *zoomorphize*!) God. They make God look like a creature of the earth. A theology in which anthropomorphism is completely accursed necessarily resists idols tooth and nail. It cannot conceive how a person or beast might image the Holy. It cannot imagine that heaven shares our needs and weaknesses. The Reverence School's assumptions exclude idols out of hand.

zoomorphize: to attribute animal form or animal attributes to what is not an animal.

The Lord is not continuous with creation, and is not dependent or contingent on it, according to the Reverence School. This comes across plainly in the school's Scriptures, particularly in its descriptions of Israel's sacrificial system. These descriptions bend over backward to keep God from looking human.

According to the Reverence School strand, sacrifices specifically do *not* satisfy the daily needs of the Lord. In contrast to other priestly texts (such as Num 28:2; Ezek 44:7), the God of this strand never calls sacrifices "my food." This sharply distinguishes the true God from idols. Near Easterners fed and watered their idols, ignorant that the Holy has no need of nourishment.

bread of the Presence: holy bread placed in the temple before God as a sacrificial offering every Sabbath.

Driving their point home, the Reverence School strand prohibits any burnt offerings, grain offerings, or drink offerings on the incense altar inside the tabernacle (Exod 30:9 RS). The strand insists that the priests must entirely consume the only food allowed inside the shrine, the bread of the Presence (Lev 24:8–9). No one must mistakenly think that God eats gifts of food.[6]

Other biblical theologies considered the temple sanctuary in Jerusalem to be God's dwelling, but not the Reverence School. In reverence theology, the Lord neither eats sacrifices nor dwells in a temple. The phrase "tabernacle of the LORD" never appears in the strand (contrast other priestly texts, such as Lev 17:4; Num 16:9; 17:13; 19:13; 31:30, 47). Neither does the Lord ever speak of the sanctuary as "my dwelling" (contrast Lev 15:31; 26:11; and Ezek 37:27). The poems of 2 Isaiah agree completely: "Thus says the LORD: Heaven is my throne and the earth is my footstool; what is the house that you would build for me, and what is my resting place?" (Isa 66:1; cf. 57:15).

Heaven is my throne and the earth is my footstool; what is the house that you would build for me? —Isa 66:1

For the Reverence School Scriptures, the sanctuary is merely a meeting place. The School uses the Hebrew verb *no'ad*, "meet at an appointed place," to describe what happens there between Israel and the Lord (Exod 25:22; 30:6, 36 RS). In no way earthbound, the Lord's glory appears at the sanctuary only intermittently, flashing forth from between the ark's two cherubim.

When the prophet Ezekiel describes the ark's cherub angels, he speaks of them supporting a "likeness" of divinity (Ezek 1:28), an image of God in "human form" (Ezek 1:26). The Reverence School Scriptures know nothing of this. In the Reverence School strand, God speaks from *between* the

cherubim: Winged sphinxes guarding God's presence, represented by statues atop the ark of the covenant (the sacred chest in the temple's inner sanctum).

47

cherub statues on the ark, not as a humanoid seated above them (e.g., Exod 25:22; 30:6, 36; Lev 16:2 RS). God's appearing is marked by opaque clouds and burning flames. There is no visible image involved whatsoever (e.g., Lev 9:23–24; 10:2; 16:2 RS).

For visual art to represent the Holy, the Reverence School claims, it must use negative means. A sense of ineffable mystery is best conveyed by pure space, vaulted absence, and eerie vacancy. The cherubim's wings in the Reverence School Scriptures frame such space, powerfully presenting us with palpable emptiness. They direct our gaze past all human experience toward the Beyond. The clear effect is a reverent suppression of anthropomorphism.

God's appearances between the cherubim communicate the divine will, making it plain to the understanding (Exod 25:22; 31:18 RS). Idolaters have to put up with vague, misleading doubletalk and mediums make do with mere whispers and moans.[7] Not the Lord's people. God's reverent servants live effectively, relying on clear, articulate revelation from heaven. There is no need for obfuscation, when your vantage lies beyond the cosmos. As director of earth's history, the Lord knows its goal and how to get our lives aligned with it.

A Conversation with Isaiah 45:18–21

We are now prepared to enjoy more conversations with the texts of 2 Isaiah. I have two passages in mind for us that combat idolatry and anthropomorphism with inspired, poetic power. Let us begin with Isaiah 45:18–21.

We will be looking at two strophes ("stanzas") of a larger poem. The first strophe presents a paradox: God, the Holy One, who dwells far beyond our mind's reach, has revealed God's self to us. God has made God's plans intelligible. The second strophe challenges idolaters to try to compete with God's revealed wisdom. They cannot, because the pantheon of gods, being continuous with creation, has no vantage for discerning life's design and goal. The Lord, in contrast, who is fully *other* than creation, has this vantage.

[18] For thus says the LORD,
who created the heavens /
(he is God!), //

who formed the earth and made it /
    (he established it; //
he did not create it a chaos, /
    he formed it to be inhabited!): //
I am the LORD, and there is no other. //
[19] I did not speak in secret, /
    in a land of darkness; //
I did not say to the offspring of Jacob, /
    "Seek me in chaos." //
I the LORD speak the truth, /
    I declare what is right. //

[20] Assemble yourselves and come together, /
    draw near, you survivors of the nations! //
They have no knowledge— /
    those who carry about their wooden idols, //
and keep on praying to a god /
    that cannot save. //
[21] Declare and present your case; /
    let them take counsel together! //
Who told this long ago? /
    Who declared it of old? //
Was it not I, the LORD? /
    There is no other god besides me, //
a righteous God and a Savior; /
    there is no one besides me. //

The poem's first half revolves around the wonder of God's self-revelation. The Hidden One has chosen not to hide! How different from the doubletalk of idolaters and the whispers of mediums. The true God, the God of mystery, elects to work in the open. We are not left in the dark, reaching out for God in vain, feeling around in some unlit corner. The God of uncanny otherness has chosen to reveal God's purposes to humanity. The Lord proclaims, "I did not speak in secret, / in a land of darkness.//"

Well, then, if God speaks in the open, *where* precisely does God speak? In what locale? Where can we find such a place of revelation, which is not "a land of darkness"? We would like to know the illumined spot the poem has in mind, where God shows forth God's purposes.

I think our poem has a specific site of revelation in mind, and subtly alludes to it. It is Jerusalem's temple, and specifically the framed emptiness between the temple's cherubim. Here, at this unique place of epiphany and light, Israel could learn God's clear, defined will.

The language of verse 19 contains the allusion that I have in mind, but the allusion is clearer when we reword the verse in positive rather than negative terms. Consider this possible rephrasing: "Yahweh has spoken in a place, he has said to the seed of Jacob '(there) seek me!'"[8] For Israel, the "place" (*maqom*) is specifically Zion and the temple in Jerusalem. The Hebrew term *maqom* often means "holy place," "sacred site."

Our next question is obvious. If God has revealed a will and a plan for us, what are they? God claims to have built the world with such a plan in mind. The plan is no secret, it is claimed, but has long been openly and intelligibly revealed. God did not create the earth "a chaos" (v. 18), and God does not expect us to search out its design "in chaos" (v. 19). Very good; how do we get clear about this design?

Look at the poem more closely. When it states that God did not create the world a chaos but "formed it to be inhabited," it presents us with another subtle allusion. An echo of Genesis 1:28 and the primal blessing is hard to miss. God's command in Genesis was to "fill the earth." God brought the earth out of chaos to become a home—a robust, vibrant, praising home. According to 2 Isaiah, God's new redemptive work will finally bring this plan to fruition. Earth will finally become a habitation after God's own heart, just as planned in Genesis, filled with those who sing God's praise in awe and reverence.

Now let's turn to our poem's second strophe, in verses 20–21. We shift abruptly to a courtroom scene, with earth's idolaters on trial. They gather for litigation in the wake of the international campaigns of King Cyrus of Persia. The time is ripe to see who is right about life and the course of history. Is it the idolaters or the followers of the Holy One of Israel?

The imagery and language of a law court helps the community of 2 Isaiah get people thinking. They are always trying to get their audience to put their heads together and look at the facts. "Use your brain!" is their mantra; consider history, prophecy, and the rise and fall of empires.

Notice all the questions in verse 21. Prosecutors' questions get a jury attentive, mentally engaged. They interrogate and cross-examine their witnesses in order to root out the truth. "Make your case!" "What deity is able to make sense of life?" It is certainly *not* the idols of Babylon. "Look at the evidence: It can only be the Lord. It has to be Yahweh!"

Nations rise and fall, battles are lost and won, but God's verbal revelation stands reliable. There is no future for Babylonia's proud spirit; its hold over God's people can have no staying power. The Lord's prophets saw it long ago. They announced it when Babylonia was still off everyone's radar, and no one had heard of Cyrus of Persia.

Take the prophet Habakkuk. God showed him the downfall of Babylonia far in advance. The rise of Cyrus could have held no surprise to him. What did astound him was the mystery of God's person and work. At his vision of the Holy One, he shivered with awe and felt himself undone. "Rottenness enters into my bones," he wrote, "and my steps tremble beneath me. I wait quietly for the day of calamity to come upon the people [the Babylonians] who attack us" (Hab 3:16).

The center of the second strophe comes at the end of verse 20. Babylonia's idols "cannot save." Salvific power belongs exclusively to the Lord, because of who God is. The God of 2 Isaiah both transcends history, planning its course, and works openly within it, making plain the path to joy.

By contrast, the puppet-gods are immanent within creation, having no vantage outside it. The course of history leaves them puzzled. They do not know how to get things right; they do not know how to help. Their worshipers are ignorant: "They

The God of 2 Isaiah both transcends history, planning its course, and works openly within it, making plain the path to joy.

have no knowledge" (v. 20). They strut and fret with their wooden idols, clinging to their empty claims like addicts in a stupor.

The Mesopotamian pantheon is moored to worship images, circumscribed by blocks of wood—mere dead sticks! Derivative of the ebb and flow of the cosmos, these gods were bound up in the world even before their worship images were crafted. Even if they could save us, even if they were in touch with history's course, the Babylonian gods would likely do us no favors. According to Babylonian myth, the gods Marduk and Ea created us for selfish purposes, out of a desire for slaves. "These aborigines will do the divine assembly's work," they proposed. "These savages will set the divine assembly free."[9]

As originally conceived by Marduk and Ea, humans were meant to serve the gods, setting them free from labor. The gods have no plan to illumine humanity, to guide them toward ennoblement. If mortals desire illumination, they must settle for the omens and portents of diviners or the whispers and moans of the dead.

How different is the creator God, who formed human beings in the divine image and destined them to bloom and spread. God has made God's self available to humanity, ready to be found, ready to direct us to a robust, effective, praising life. One strains to imagine the grace of the Lord.

The court trial ends with a clear verdict. "There is no other god besides me," the Lord declares, "a righteous God and a Savior; there is no one besides me" (v. 21). Strikingly, the verdict leads not to a judgment on the idolaters but to a universal offer of salvation. From the beginning, the Reverence School purposed to spread God's salvation to the multitude of nations (Gen 17:4–6). That purpose flowers here in God's offer to the world: "Turn to me and be saved, all the ends of the earth! For I am God, and there is no other" (v. 22).

A Conversation with Isaiah 46:1–4

A second poem, Isaiah 46:1–4, takes on idolatry, pride, and ignorance from another angle: that of humor. It taunts the gods of Babylonia, ripe for defeat before Cyrus's armies. It then turns to the Lord's total and unique sovereignty and commitment to God's people.

The scene is the near future. Babylon's fate is sealed and its idols are being carted off. The once proud worship images used to ride triumphantly down canals on barges and through the streets of the capital in New Year's processions. Now, they journey humiliated into exile on the backs of beasts of burden.

Bel is an honorific title, meaning "lord" or "master," and here designates Marduk, Babylon's patron deity. The god *Nebo* was Marduk's son, who, along with his father, had a leading role in the New Year's festival. His sacred barge would arrive to much rejoicing in the capital city, his father's home. After disembarking, he and Marduk would preside over rites purifying the city and temple and bolstering the unity and hopes of the nation.

Isaiah 46:1–4 reads as follows:

¹ Bel bows down, Nebo stoops, /
    their idols are on beasts and cattle; //
these things you carry are loaded /
    as burdens on weary animals. //
² They stoop, they bow down together; /
    they cannot save the burden, /
    but themselves go into captivity. //

³ Listen to me, O house of Jacob, /
    all the remnant of the house of Israel, //
who have been borne by me from your birth, /
    carried from the womb; //
⁴ even to your old age I am he, /
    even when you turn gray I will carry you. //
I have made, and I will bear; /
    I will carry and will save. //

This poem is a prime specimen of the pure, marvelous wit of 2 Isaiah's poetry. It is superb, daring satire. Babylonia's no-god blocks of wood are completely ridiculous deities, and our authors do not hesitate to drive that point home. The entities that were supposed to bear people's cares and troubles are instead "loaded as burdens on weary animals." Burdens cannot bear burdens. Far from uplifting their servitors, idols are only one more thing to lug around. Feel sad for the poor mules! Now that Babylonia has met its defeat in Persia, the beasts have to carry off this dead weight.

As we read the poem, we can picture Babylon's idols swaying back and forth precariously atop the beasts' overloaded backs. "Bel bows down, Nebo stoops." Wearily, the mules stagger ahead, no doubt puzzling at the stupidity of their masters who once worshiped these things. What a contrast to the elaborate New Year's parades of recent memory, when the bejeweled, royally vested icons processed in glory. What delicious irony!

But, wait a minute. Can this sort of language be called reverent? The term *irreverence* seems more apt! To the surprise of many, reverence does not oppose wit, satire, and mockery. Indeed, reverent folk may be first to burst out laughing at haughty claims and ridiculous pomposity. Keenly aware of the truth of human frailty, reverence often simply cannot suppress guffaws at foolish pretenders and mighty dupes.[10]

Twice our poem uses the verbs "bow down" and "stoop/cower" with reference to Bel-Marduk and Nebo. As we move from the beginning of verse 1 to the start of verse 2, the order of the verbs is reversed. The skillful poetic repetition and reverse ordering of the words highlights the shame of the gods. Indeed, a major purpose of all this uproarious mockery is to create an air of shame about idolatry.

If one feels shame, reverence is not far behind. To feel shame is to be conscious of shortcomings or improprieties over against something larger, something overarching. To acknowledge something larger and overarching, however, is to find oneself backing into reverence. Reverence arises precisely as one recognizes some greater standard that dwarfs the self.

The second strophe of our poem (vv. 3–4) opens with the divine command "Listen to me." It is 2 Isaiah's characteristic summons to engage our minds, to hear God out. "Why not consider accepting—even embracing—your human finitude?" God suggests. All it takes is a renewed sense of humor and a healing dose of humility. And God will be there to make things right.

The coherent basis of the strophe is the clause "I am he." We could equally render the Hebrew "I am it." Completely unlike the gods of Babylon, Israel's God is not reduced, managed, or externally controlled. The Lord is the only game in town, totally and uniquely holy, lone in grandeur, lone in glory. Count the number of "I"s in verse 4. God repeats the pronoun "I" (Hebrew *'ani*) no less than five times. Positively and earnestly,

The Lord is the only game in town, totally and uniquely holy, lone in grandeur, lone in glory.

God asserts God's absolute divine prerogative in existence. God's unique holiness gives God that prerogative.

The effect of the multiple pronouns in verse 4 is compounded in the Hebrew, where the verb forms also communicate a first-person subject. The Hebrew literally reads, "*I, I* will carry," "*I, I* have made," "*I, I* will bear," "*I, I* will carry," and "*I* will save."

God's assertion "I will save" is the final, climactic "I"-statement of the series. It is the poem's last word and its whole point. It reaches back in contrast with its antithesis in the first strophe. There, verse 2 made clear that Marduk and Nebo cannot protect the people, "cannot save" anyone. In contrast, the Lord certainly can, and will.

Just consider the saving history of Israel; consider the story of the exodus. An idol does not answer or save anyone from trouble, but Israel has been borne and carried from the beginning, from its birth. God has been there for the people all along, guiding and saving them. This work, "from the womb," has been done out in the open. Pharaoh's magicians saw the finger of God at Israel's emergence as a people, and they trembled.

Strophe one and strophe two of our poem present two alternative forms of life. Strophe one (vv. 1–2) is about loading oneself down with the gods, scrabbling and puddering to and fro in the manner of Superbia. Strophe two (vv. 3–4) is about reposing in the Lord, letting the Lord bear one up. The contrast is a simple one: spirituality as a lift versus spirituality as a load; divinity as wings versus divinity as weights; devotion as buoyancy versus devotion as befuddlement.

Strophe one speaks of the gods of idolatry as "these things you carry," things that are "loaded/borne as burdens" (v. 1). Strophe two presents an opposite perspective: divinity's mysterious desire to carry *us*. It drives home the mystery with no less than five different assertions, beginning with two passive participles in verse 3.

Israel has been "borne by me," God reminds the people (v 3). They have been "carried from the womb" (v. 3). These are the same two Hebrew verbs as in verse 1, but in reverse order. The verbal artistry is effective. It poetically exposes idolatry and turns its claims on their head. The Lord is a God who turns the tables on the opposition.

As for the future, God promises: "I, I will carry you" (v. 4), and repeats, "I, I will bear"; "I, I will carry" (v. 4). Here, a new verb appears, meaning "carry an especially heavy burden" (Hebrew *sabal*). No degree of weightiness will ever dissuade God from God's purposes. God's commitment to bear us up is superlative.

Because the Lord is other, uniquely holy and lone in glory, God's nature is simply incompatible with burdening humanity. Supplying the needs of the Lord or carrying the Lord's cares is completely out of the question for us. God's self-dependence, however, does not spell God's isolation. The Lord is no god of dualism or mysticism. To the contrary, God is permanently, lovingly, and selflessly engaged with God's people. We cannot help but feel precious in God's active, tangible embrace.

Reverence theology upholds an unconditional, unilateral covenant based solely on God's steadfast love. Here, that love is palpable. God has been there, carrying Israel from the day they were born. God will be there, carrying them still, when they are old and gray. God's promises here really move us, much like a love letter.

What a contrast with Babylonian polytheism! The pantheon of gods brought forth humans as slaves to do their work, to set the gods free. Marduk specifically declares as much in making humankind. He wants to supply his fellow gods with slaves that they might have ease. Such things as love and commitment are far from his mind.

Whereas Marduk made humankind to relieve the gods' burdens, the Lord acted for the opposite reason. God made people in order to bear *them* up, to carry *them* toward ennoblement. "Be fruitful and multiply," God blessed God's people. "Fill the earth" (Gen 1:28 RS).

Meditate with me a moment on this wondrous desire of God to bear us, to gather us in and carry us in the divine bosom. I believe that in discovering this divine desire, we have hit upon what 2 Isaiah considers to be God's central yearning for humanity, a yearning for the collapse of pride.

Pride is alienation from God, turning away from God to focus on the self. The ideal of 2 Isaiah is the opposite: it wants us to find true joy reposing in God's wonder and care. It wants us to relax, let go, and let God bear and carry us.

God's *otherness* makes self-surrender a breeze. No one, not even the fantastically gorgeous Narcissus,[11] could obsess with the self in the face of the Holy. Even a glimmer of the haunting otherness of

God in his reflecting pool would have shocked Narcissus out of his narcotic trance. His personal beauty—his idol—could no longer chain him. One cannot remain self-absorbed in the presence of the completely *other*. A flashlight holds no interest in broad daylight.

> *One cannot remain self-absorbed in the presence of the completely* other. *A flashlight holds no interest in broad daylight.*

Reposed in God's bosom, in God's awesome otherness, we can surrender our selves in the manner of lovers enraptured with their partners. Like a lover, we can give up our self to our beloved, finding real happiness as our center of concern shifts away from our ego to the wonder of the sublime.

The metaphor of lovemaking is helpful, because good lovemaking evokes a tangible reverence and pushes back pride. Surely, love making gives many modern people one of their few tastes of an encounter with the Holy. It attests to the positive value of surrendering the self. Once we have met the Holy, we find ourselves without ego and intensely desire such surrender.

Continuing the Conversation . . .

Though some of its allusions are obscure or dated, you may enjoy C. S. Lewis's allegorical fantasy of an intellectual journey toward Christianity, *The Pilgrim's Regress: An Allegorical Apology for Christianity, Reason, and Romanticism* (New York: Bantam, 1943).

For a lucid exploration of God's primal blessing of creation in the Reverence School strand, see Walter Brueggemann, "Chapter 6: The Kerygma of the Priestly Writers," in Walter Brueggemann and Hans Walter Wolff, *The Vitality of Old Testament Traditions*, 2nd ed. (Atlanta: John Knox, 1982), 101–13.

Servanthood and the Exuberance of the Holy

Grant us, O Lord, to trust in you with all our hearts; for as you always resist the proud who confide in their own strength, so you never forsake those who make their boast of your mercy.

COLLECT FOR PROPER 18,
THE EPISCOPAL *BOOK OF COMMON PRAYER*

In the preceding chapter, we took a long, hard look at idolatry and pride. Idolatry's perverse effect, we discovered, is to entangle us in the tangible and the contingent, to wrap us up in the known, familiar world of human technique and manipulation. In so doing, it whisks us away into estrangement from God, the divine Other (Isa 48:4–5). Idols alienate us from ourselves as well, for our identity as human beings can only mature as we give ourselves up to God, our creator.

Most of us are largely unaware that anything is wrong with our everyday, slip-sliding way of life, which knows little of God's succor and turns ever more single-mindedly toward self concern. A constant assertion of the self comes naturally to us from birth. There are some of us, of course, who willingly share our talents and resources, making meaningful sacrifices on behalf of others. There are few indeed, however, who deliberately dethrone the self, permanently relinquish the driver's seat, and let God lead.

In his powerful prayers, Søren Kierkegaard (1813–1855), the celebrated Danish theologian, drives home the point. He writes, "It is certainly true that there are some acts which the human language particularly and narrow-mindedly calls acts of charity; but in heaven it is certainly true that no act can be pleasing unless it is an act of love: sincere in its self-abnegation."[1]

Dominion over one's self feels normal. Preserving and promoting our personal well-being, our integrity, and our interests is practically a moral reflex for us. Yet, at least according to a theology of reverence, this reflex is ultimately ineffective and abortive. The self is not Self. It cannot flourish thrown back upon moral independence and narcissism (Isa 47:8, 10; 50:11).

In the spiritual classic *The Knowledge of the Holy,* A. W. Tozer writes:

> Eight hundred years before the advent of Christ the prophet Isaiah identified sin as . . . the assertion of the right of each man to choose for himself the way he shall go. "All we like sheep have gone astray," he said, "we have turned every one to his own way" [Isa 53:6], and I believe that no more accurate description of sin has ever been given.[2]

A(iden) W(ilson) Tozer: an American Protestant pastor, preacher, and author (1897–1963).

The form of life opposite to idolatry, pride, and sin, according to 2 Isaiah, is servanthood. Instead of straining our capacities, leaving us spent, the servant lifestyle strangely imbues us with power. Peculiarly empowered as God's servants, we do not need to become lean and exhausted in life. We can break free from the chains of ignorance and pride. Servanthood, 2 Isaiah claims, is the paradoxical path to life as it was meant to be lived. It is the surprising means of becoming real, of actualizing one's true personhood. A genuine servant lives exuberantly, called by God's name, created for God's glory.

The ideal of servanthood rings through the poems of 2 Isaiah. Recognize that you are a dependent and contingent being, our texts implore the reader. Over against the Holy, you are a tiny "grasshopper" (Isa 40:22), a feeble "worm," a fragile "insect" (Isa 41:14). You are too frail to go it alone. If you can just accept your finitude, 2 Isaiah suggests, you will never be so smug as to consider yourself "Number One."

"All people are grass, their constancy is like the flower of the field," Isaiah's poetry proffers (Isa 40:6; cf. 51:12; 53:2). And, like grass, human life flourishes only in mutuality and community. Grass is supposed to carpet the earth, not subsist as isolated blades or shriveled clippings. It is supposed to transform wastelands into oases, into fresh, verdant fields (Isa 44:3–5; 45:8).

> All people are grass, their constancy is like the flower of the field. —Isa 40:6

From the time of creation, God has been at work fashioning humanity into a rolling, blanketing meadowland—a well-watered, thriving meadow of persons in relation (cf. Isa 58:10–11; 61:11). God's work has been to shape humanity into a support network of interrelated brothers and sisters, sharing the same surname (Isa 44:5). If we all bear the name "the Lord's" in common, we have to care about each other. We have to live together in shalom and mutual service, not in chaos as isolated monads (Isa 45:18; 56:7; 59:8; 65:25).

Mutual service includes generous kindness, giving oneself to the down-and-out, to those on the periphery (cf. Isa 42:3, 7; 47:6; 49:8–9; 58:7; 61:1). Thus, Isaiah 58:10 proclaims, "If you offer your food to the hungry and satisfy the needs of the afflicted, then your light shall rise in the darkness and your gloom be like the noonday."

Being a servant of God further entails breaking down artificial barriers. According to 2 Isaiah, serving the God of Holiness means reaching out to the foreigner, to the other (Isa 45:14, 22; 49:6; 55:5; 56:3; 66:20–21).

More than mere ministers to the needy, however, the ideal servants of 2 Isaiah are agents and confidants of the Lord. As the text makes clear, God wants the entire Israelite community collectively to become the "servant of the Lord." They are to be God's specially appointed representative on earth, who performs God's work in the midst of humanity. (For Israel directly termed God's "servant" [Hebrew 'ebed], see Isa 41:8–9; 42:19; 43:10; 44:1–2, 21; 45:4; and 48:20.)

Israel's role as the servant of the Lord involves bearing God's blessing, becoming a fruitful and prosperous people of God. God's people are to think big and branch out. Their directive is to spread reverence as a form of life, spread it abroad to the right and to the left (Isa 44:3–4).

Their servant role further entails bearing witness to God, presenting evidence to the world that the Lord is the only savior there is. Based on the reality of their entire history, Israel must testify before the nations of God's presence in its life. "You are my witnesses, says the LORD, and my servant whom I have chosen" (Isa 43:10; cf. 44:8).

Ultimately, the redeemed Israel is to represent the Lord by showcasing God's holy glory. Consider the promise of Isaiah 44:23, which reads in part, "Break forth into singing, O mountains, O forest, and every tree in it! For the LORD has redeemed Jacob, and will be glorified in Israel" (cf. Isa 43:7; 49:3; 55:5; 60:9, 21; 61:3; 62:3).

God's Preferential Option for the Downtrodden

Becoming servants of the Lord, letting God dethrone the self, is almost certainly easiest for those walloped by misfortune, those at the end of their rope. The Babylonian exiles addressed by 2 Isaiah were assuredly in this position (e.g., Isa 42:7, 22; 49:21).

Poor-in-spirit folk are oddly fortunate, it seems, for it may not be as much of a struggle for them to humbly take up the Lord's service. Well in touch with their spiritual poverty, they have little or no ego to get in the way of God reigning over their lives. Jesus said it well in Matthew 5:3, "God blesses those who are poor and realize their need for him" (NLT). Or as one paraphrase of the verse reads, "With less of you there is more of God and his rule" (THE MESSAGE).

Those cast down by life have a strange spiritual advantage. The humble and uncertain have the least problem admitting to something larger than themselves, something before which every person stands puny and profane. They are ideally primed to recognize their frailty, feel awe before the Holy, and know reverence. It is but a small step for them to turn their human frailty into power, to grasp onto servanthood as a means to victory. Their pride already gone, they are predisposed to throw themselves on God's grace. And God greets them with open arms, wants them all back, every last one called by God's name (e.g., Isa 43:7; 50:10; 54:6–8; 55:1–2, 7). What an enigma! The lowly and downtrodden have preferential access to the high and towering One.

Isaiah 66:1–2 affirms that the lowly and open-spirited are closest to God's wondrous embrace[3]:

Thus says the LORD:
Heaven is my throne
    and the earth is my footstool;
what is the house that you would build for me,
    and what is my resting place?
All these things my hand has made,
    and so all these things are mine,
        says the LORD.
But this is the one to whom I will look,
    to the humble and contrite in spirit,
    who trembles at my word.

Isaiah 57:15 makes the identical point: God occupies time without end and heights without limit but is most at home with the crushed and dejected in spirit:

> The high and lofty one who lives in eternity, the Holy One, says this: "I live in the high and holy place [yet also] with those whose spirits are contrite and humble. I restore the crushed spirit of the humble and revive the courage of those with repentant hearts." (NLT)

Whether or not we are physically downtrodden, we must all live out of our innate spiritual poverty, 2 Isaiah's poetry avers. We must latch onto servanthood. We must respect all human persons and commit to living with others in mutual service. This is the only viable lifestyle for effective existence within human history.

The Exaltation of Servanthood

Selflessness and service yield existential power. It flows mysteriously out of other-centered commitment to God and neighbor. Our strength lies in taking ourselves much less seriously, and focusing instead on God and the needs of others.

Throughout the centuries of church history, perhaps no one understood this better than Francis of Assisi (1182–1226). "God grant that I may seek not so much to be loved, as to love," Francis is said to have prayed. "It is in giving that we receive," he continued. This brief declaration brings us to the heart of the power of the servant lifestyle (cf. Luke 14:12; Acts 20:35). The

Francis of Assisi: Italian friar who founded the Franciscan order (1182–1226).

paraphrase of this prayer by James Quinn (Hymn 593 in *The Hymnal 1982*) beautifully captures Francis's thought: "May we not look for love's return, but seek to love unselfishly, for in giving we receive, and in forgiving are forgiven." It is only in seeking to love unselfishly that we receive true abundance.

Kierkegaard knew the same truth. Authentic love makes no claims and achieves no merit, but instead practices self-sacrifice and self-denial. Cutting out our self-focus and cutting ourselves down to size is the means of letting God's goodness in. "God in Heaven, let me really feel my nothingness," Kierkegaard prayed, "not in order to despair over it, but in order to feel the more powerfully the greatness of Thy goodness."[4]

> Cutting out our self-focus and cutting ourselves down to size is the means of letting God's goodness cut in.

As servanthood spreads throughout human communities on earth, each servant, in turn, finds herself or himself selflessly served by others. In this way, every servant-disciple indirectly discovers the affirmation for which he or she longs. They experience the unconditional love of those around them, lose their instinctual fears, and abandon their chains of self-concern. What is more, the servant-faithful are led to God's nurturing bosom and the fundamental empowerment that lies there. They come into sync with the Holy, finding themselves reborn in its energy. Suddenly, they find their feet grounded, their heads lifted high. God states, "See, my servant shall prosper; he shall be exalted and lifted up, and shall be very high" (Isa 52:13). This is also God's message: "Whoever takes refuge in me shall possess the land and inherit my holy mountain" (Isa 57:13).[5]

We have seen the power that even a modicum of reverence brought King Cyrus of Persia. Because Cyrus embraced his finitude and vulnerability, he was able to build a great empire. His subjects felt their dignity respected under his reign. Under a comparatively reverent rule, they had no reason to plot violence and rebellion. Rather than seethe in humiliation and frustration, they had good cause for loyalty.

Where reverence abounds, leaders and followers experience a sense of shared endeavor. They see themselves united in serving a lofty purpose, something higher than any one of them. In this sense, they find themselves morally and profoundly equal to one another.[6] They are "equal" in their awe-inspired devotion to what transcends them. Feeling this way, sharing a profound reverence, they respect each other fulsomely. In fact, they may wholeheartedly commit to each other.

Cyrus, we believe, never knew an elevated level of reverence, leading the soul in ever more intense, sacrificial directions. He never directly encountered the Holy One of Israel, certainly never contemplated a spiritual rebirth in God's bosom. One can only imagine how much more Cyrus might have achieved if he had pushed farther with his fledgling religious insights.

Let me briefly hypothesize about the nature and roots of the powerful exaltation experienced in a selfless repose in God, the sort of repose never experienced by Cyrus. For this purpose, I can use the metaphor of a line or circle dance. I will be able to develop my suggestions in this and the subsequent chapter, when we ruminate on the profound poetry of Isaiah 50:4–11, 52:13–53:12, and 40:27–31.

It appears to me that a direct experience of the Holy, willingly embraced, throws the soul into a great, wondrous dance. The primary dance partner is God, but others are on the dance floor, God's human collaborators. The dance begins as our human selves deflate and take on boundaries. Thus circumscribed, each ego has space freed up around it for encounters and intimate interactions with God and other selves.

Once our imagined "dance of spirituality" begins, the participants immediately feel its throbbing energy. All are buoyed up by its flowing rhythms, synchronized moves, and dizzying interactions. The dance is intimate, dynamic, and, above all, synergistic. All are enmeshed in a great, flowing expansion of spirit.

What is the meaning of this dance? To what do I refer? I am striving to elaborate the sort of interchange between God and God's servants entailed in a text such as Isaiah 40:31. The reverent keep walking and running, according to the verse, but all the while, they are receiving new wind, fresh strength. Ideally attuned to their exertions, God is continually refreshing their vigor.

> Those who wait for the LORD shall renew their strength, they shall mount up with wings like eagles, they shall run and not be weary, they shall walk and not faint.
> —Isa 40:31

Reading this verse, I envision ecstatic adoration and service flowing selflessly up to God from God's servants. From there, love's power immediately and uninterruptedly flows back to God's people in the form of being, shalom, and joy—all free gifts. Actually, we should imagine the cycle beginning neither on earth nor in heaven. In its perfect form, it is a continuous interchange of love, an unbroken circuit of power.

CLEARING AWAY MISPERCEPTIONS

Words such as "servanthood" and "submission" are highly problematic these days. Some misunderstand servanthood to involve masochistic and self-destructive tendencies. Others, equally confused, believe the notion provides oppressors a convenient alibi for artificial inequities and hurtful discriminations.

Reverence theology, it is true, does question our modern ideological touting of human autonomy, but only out of a steadfast conviction about where true joy is to be found. A preoccupation with self-determination, our theology claims, leads inevitably to slavery. Only dethroning and surrendering the self allows God the working room to nurture our full humanity and personhood.

The notions of "servants" and "servanthood" have a specialized and developed meaning in 2 Isaiah. A particular servant role, borrowed from elsewhere in Scripture, is central to our poems: the role of royal attendant. When you see the term "servant" in our texts, you should think primarily of a privileged steward, a royal confidant. As we shall see, that understanding helps clear up many misimpressions.

Far from menials, royal servants of the Bible were the king's agents and emissaries. Securely embedded in the royal court and household, they possessed significant delegated authority and were joyous beneficiaries of a monarch's largesse. Crown lands and shares in tax revenue often accrued to them as rewards for their loyalty and service (cf. 1 Sam 8:14–15).

In the Hebrew Scriptures, earthly monarchs have a variety of royal attendants but so also does God. "The King, the LORD of hosts" (Isa 6:5; cf. 43:15; 44:6) has many "servants," who, like the attendants of terrestrial monarchs, have access to their lord's council and serve as their lord's representatives and mediators. Since they take up God's cause, carrying out God's work, servants of the Lord may be considered "apprentices" of God. Like disciples of a master practitioner, they strive to promote and embody their mentor's ideals and purposes.

If the word "servant" is offensive to you, try substituting the word "apprentice." In interpreting 2 Isaiah, we can equally speak of *apprentice theology* as of *servant theology*. 2 Isaiah's servants are those who open their ears daily to God's instruction, who "give heed like disciples" (Isa 50:4 NJPS). They are ready to take orders, confident that dogged surrender to the Holy is not wimpish but the way to get life right (Isa 50:7).

> **Abraham:** the first of the Old Testament ancestors, the founder of the Hebrew people through his son Isaac and grandson Jacob.

Far from an embarrassing or degrading role, persons designated "servants of the LORD" in the Bible often claim God's special call and blessing. Abraham and David are particularly prominent servants of the Lord in this sense, since both bore in their persons an eternal promise of God. Both became channels of God to bless Israel and, through Israel, all of creation.

Repeatedly, in Israel's story, God sustains the people because of eternal divine promises made to God's servants Abraham and David. Thus, Psalm 105:42 links God's care of Israel after the exodus with God's remembering "his holy promise, and Abraham, his *servant*" (emphasis added). Similarly, God keeps a steady, protective hand on Jerusalem because of a promise to God's servant David. When the armies of Assyria threaten Jerusalem, God vows, "I will defend this city to save it, for my own sake and for the sake of my *servant* David" (2 Kgs 19:34; emphasis added). These two examples explicitly link servanthood with bearing God's fail-safe promise to bring blessing to earth.

> **David:** a Hebrew shepherd who founded Judah's great royal dynasty, which God endowed with eternal promises.

The Servant of the Lord in 2 Isaiah

The most dramatic presentations of servanthood in 2 Isaiah occur in a group of passages that scholars call the *Servant Songs*. These poems about an ideal Servant of the Lord include Isaiah 42:1–4; 49:1–6; 50:4–9; 52:13–53:12; and 61:1–3. They are difficult texts to interpret; in fact, they are among the most controversial passages of Scripture.

Israel as a whole is considered God's "servant" in 2 Isaiah, as we have seen. From the time of Abraham, Isaiah 41:8 declares, God specially chose the Israelite people as personal attendants and confidants. In the Servant Songs, however, matters shift noticeably. These intriguing poems understand the identity of God's servant differently, in a way that precludes identifying him with all Israel.

A "collective" understanding of the hero of the Servant Songs, though commonplace, is untenable. The persistent individual language that the songs apply to their protagonist is hard to dismiss. The Suffering Servant simply does not strike the reader as the personification of the Judean exiles. He always speaks as an "I," or "me," or is referred to as a "he." Further, he lives life in a remarkable, counterintuitive manner that sets him apart from everyone around him, making him a unique, peculiar specimen. He makes a one-of-a-kind sacrifice of his life, which "makes the many righteous" (Isa 53:11 NJPS).

The Servant Songs distinguish their hero markedly from the communal body of God's people. Most impressively, the Servant's moral nature differs from that of his contemporaries like day from night. Unlike the Israelite nation as a whole, which has been exiled due to sin and transgression (Isa 50:1), the Servant has led an attentive, obedient life (Isa 50:5). To the end, he lives unblemished and blameless before God (Isa 53:5). He dies without any taint of violence or deceit (Isa 53:9).

What is more, the Servant is clearly on a mission to deliver the rest of his country folk (e.g., Isa 53:4–6). God is commissioning him "to bring Jacob back," appointing him "that Israel might be gathered" (Isa 49:5). He is God's example for his people to follow and their designated leader. Presented with him by the Lord, they must choose whether to accept him (Isa 50:10–11).

While clearly not an ordinary, everyday Israel, the Servant does reveal an exemplary Israel, an Israel that fits with God's hopes. In him, God realizes all that God has ever planned for the chosen people. He brings blessing and justice to earth, never looking back until the job is done (Isa 42:4).

"*You* are now Israel," God tells the Servant in Isaiah 49:3. "You are to set in motion all of my expectations for my beloved people." Furthermore, God declares that "in you I will be glorified"; that is, "through you, I will shine" (I am paraphrasing here). Remarkable! This extraordinary hero of the Servant Songs embodies Israel in its ideal form. He accomplishes what the Israelite nation had heretofore been unable to do. He ushers in divine blessing and true harmony on earth.

Who could this intriguing figure be? Over the years, interpreters have spilled a lot of ink trying to identify the Servant with an individual figure of history. With little persuasiveness, they have suggested a complete inventory of biblical personalities. Hezekiah, Jeremiah, Cyrus, and Zerubbabel have all made it onto this list. So has the hypothetical ("reconstructed") figure who many hold first prophesied the oracles of Isaiah 40–55: "Deutero-Isaiah."

> This extraordinary hero of the Servant Songs embodies Israel in its ideal form. He accomplishes what the Israelite nation had heretofore been unable to do.

The problem has been that none of the figures on any proposed inventory fits the ideal traits of the hero of the Servant Songs. These figures were powerful human instruments of the Lord, but none combined the best features of Abraham, David, and all the prophets. None ever experienced the radical vindication and the stunning successes of the songs' protagonist. None ever experienced God's vindication on the far side of the grave (Isa 53:9–10). None ever guided history to a messianic era and "established justice in the earth" (Isa 42:4). All historic personages of the exilic era lived and died without transforming human community in the way the Servant Songs envision.

If either Cyrus or some anonymous poet or prophet is the Servant of the Lord, the Servant Songs are blatantly false prophecies that would have been found unworthy of preservation when their claims were disconfirmed. We could not have them before us today as a key part of Scripture.

I doubt that the community of faith would have treasured and preserved the Servant Songs if they believed a contemporary figure to be their protagonist. Unless these songs point beyond Cyrus and his contemporaries, their claims are either false or absurd. The songs must direct our attention beyond all historical figures from exilic times to some greater, ideal figure.

A Responsible Approach to the Servant Songs

I recommend approaching the Servant Songs as theological and spiritual meditations. Their hero is no figure of history but an artistic study. What we have here is a superb portrait of ideal servanthood.

The portrait did not emerge out of thin air, but echoes preceding Scriptures, especially the Bible's courageous servants of old. One can justly speak of the Servant as old Abraham himself. The Servant is also Sarah, David, and Jeremiah. He is the best of all of these figures, merged into one person.

The poets who created the Servant Songs must have studied and prayed long and hard over Israel's Scriptures. Out of scriptural building blocks, they constructed a figure who encapsulates the Bible's highest aspirations for human nature. In the Suffering Servant, they present us with an ideal human being in the true image of God, who holds nothing back but gives everything in love.

The language of the songs describing the Suffering Servant is radically *open* to the future. Rather than expressing one person's ancient, dusty religious experience, it empowers readers of all time to live in a radically new way. This is poetic language with power, seeking to incarnate itself in anyone willing to embrace it.

When you ruminate on the language of the Servant Songs, do not imagine the experience of some long dead hero. Imagine the ideals to which every human being, including yourself, should aspire. The ideals of the Servant Songs should be like fertilizer, able to be spread over wide tracks of land, empowering abundant new growth.

Nathaniel Hawthorne: American author of classic novels and many short stories (1804–1864).

Allow me to develop what I see to be the work of the Servant Songs by referring to a well-loved short story. In Nathaniel Hawthorne's tale "The Great Stone Face," a man named Ernest hopes throughout his life to see the prophesied incarnation of a majestic natural wonder. That wonder, the Great Stone Face, had been sculpted by wind, rain, snow, and time out of the mountainside rocks overlooking the New Hampshire valley where Ernest grew up.

As a little boy, Ernest heard from his mother an ageless prophecy to the effect that a local child would someday grow up to resemble exactly the stone face—the old man of the mountain—and would embody the virtues visible in its countenance. Ernest venerated the stone face and ruminated on the virtues it projected. As he gazed and meditated on it, the sentiments he saw in the face enlarged his heart, molded his soul. He longed to see the prophecy about the face fulfilled, blessing humanity with the sort of grand, awful, and kindly presence he saw in the facial features of the powerful rocky visage.

Ernest's ruminations on the stone face were so deep, and his hopes for a great good for humankind so broad, that the old man's love, available to all in the valley below, accrued particularly to him. Repeatedly, he saw through the pretensions of a string of claimants to fulfill the ageless prophecy he had learned as a child. At the same time, people around him began to gravitate toward him and his pure wisdom and compelling manner of life.

Eventually, to Ernest's dismay, a sensitive poet shouted out for all to hear that Ernest himself looks just like the old man of the mountain. He had put on the likeness of the towering countenance that he had admired for so long. The Great Stone Face had become incarnate in our story's hero.

The work of the Servant Songs is precisely that of the Great Stone Face. Those who revere the Songs' ideals and long for their concrete realization begin to experience inner transformation. The poems powerfully mold their committed souls. The ideal character of the Servant, full of reverence and virtue, slowly but surely takes root in their lives.

The Ideal of Servanthood in the Reverence School

2 Isaiah takes its cue on the ideal of servanthood from the Scriptures of the Reverence School. For starters, Isaiah's portrait of the Suffering Servant appears to have its primary inspiration in the Reverence School narratives of Abraham. Like the Suffering Servant, Abraham is the ideal servant and emissary of the Lord.

Abraham is God's instrument and vicar, humbly serving the intentions of God for blessing earth in its entirety. Like the Servant (Isa 42:6; 49:6), he is a force for transformation among the nations. God's covenant with Abraham in Genesis 17 (RS) starkly reveals this purpose.

In Genesis 17:4–5 (RS), Abraham becomes the special servant-agent of God, commissioned to disseminate God's intentions for humanity. For this purpose, the text uses the metaphor of fatherhood. Abraham's mission is to be a father "of a multitude of nations" (Gen 17:4 RS). This does not mean that he should become a biological progenitor of nations, but that he is charged with becoming their spiritual benefactor and mentor.

Of course, the ideal of servanthood does not apply to Abraham and his descendants alone. From the beginning of time, God's ideal role for all humankind has been the role of servants of the Lord. God wants all people eventually to take up the role of God's special representatives and confidants.

From the cosmos' creation, according to the Reverence School, God appointed human beings as God's unique servants. This was no assignment doing the dirty work of the gods, as in Babylonia's mythology. Rather, God created humanity in the "image of God" (Gen 1:27 RS) to perform kingly, royal service. This was quite an honor for mere micro-beings, dwarfed by God's newly created cosmos, miniscule against God's stars, galaxies, and the immense emptiness that separates them.

Part of God's creation blessing—God's Genesis-charge—was to "fill the earth and subdue it; and have dominion" (Gen 1:28 RS). God set humanity over the newborn world as stewards, God's caretakers of every living thing. We are indeed the honored servants of God, the Reverence School texts insist. We are the privileged servants of the Lord. Though micro-beings, hardly worth God's second look, we are agents of God in charge of the divine estate.

Perhaps so as to be sure humankind's royal appointment did not go to its head, God created the Sabbath as the pinnacle of creation (Gen 2:3 RS). The Sabbath, the seventh day, is a holy day, hallowed by God, different from other days. It is a day for recognizing God's divine prerogative, for humbling ourselves before God. On this day, the priests double the daily offerings made to God at the temple (Num 28:9–10 RS).[7]

It can be no coincidence that God chose the seventh day to summon Moses inside the fiery cloud on Mount Sinai (Exod 24:15–18 RS).[8] God compelled him to enter the devouring fire alone, exposed, and at risk. The seventh day became for him a day of nakedness before God's overwhelming power, a day of waiting in complete obedience to learn God's awesome intentions.

On every Sabbath, we get a taste of what it was like for Moses to enter the cloud. We embrace awe and contrition, remembering that existence is not about *us*. Stepping back from our preoccupations, we wait on God in obedience. God has the only power and plan in the cosmos that matter, and we discover personal fulfillment only as we integrate ourselves into them.

In the wilderness, after the exodus, God worked to foster reverence and servanthood among God's people through the miracle of the provision of *manna*. The Reverence School's narrative introduces manna, the wonder bread from heaven, in Exodus 16. In response to Israel's hunger and complaints, God rains down mysterious nourishment from the skies.

Manna is a bread of human transformation, nourishing a spirit of servanthood before God. You need calm faith—servant composure—to live by this sort of food. You need to let go of your need to be in control of where your next meal is coming from. A "me-first" attitude and a call to servanthood clash head on when manna is the main course at your meals.[9]

The frost-thin manna flakes had to be collected morning by morning, before the day warmed up, for when the sun grew hot they melted (Exod 16:21 RS). Asserting human autonomy, a few of the people tested manna's properties by storing it up for the next day, but gathering a reserve supply of manna was impossible, because it became wormy and foul overnight (v. 20). Their sorry experiment revealed no means to self-sufficiency and independence, but only maggots, a terrible stench, and Moses' wrath. The old ways of Egypt—anxiety, hoarding, and rivalry proved unworkable for an Israel called to a life of vulnerability and servanthood. Stunningly, gathering more manna yielded no extra and gathering less of it left no shortfall. After each morning's collection, Israel discovered to its amazement that "those who gathered much had nothing over, and those who gathered little had no shortage." All of them found that "they gathered as much as each of them needed" (v. 18).

> The old ways of Egypt—anxiety, hoarding, and rivalry—proved unworkable for an Israel called to a life of vulnerability and servanthood.

Living by manna—embracing servanthood—means living a life of balance and harmony with others. With manna as their food, neighbors live together in trust and vulnerability. As servants of God and of each other, neighbors develop no outrageous inequities, no dominating hierarchies, and no systems of oppression. Greed and jealousy cannot rear their ugly heads, even for a day.

Manna is obviously a bread of glad dependence and shared fellowship. The narrative of the Reverence School takes the time to describe its unique nature because it so prizes human friendship and mutuality. All God's good gifts to us, like manna, are for the sake of genuine human community, for the sake of shalom, the Reverence School avers.

Without mutual trust and vulnerability, we risk jealousy and rivalry, which can only breed violence. Violence, in turn, breeds vengeance and still more violence. It easily becomes a contagion, wreaking havoc on human community. Violence is the anti-community sin. Of all that could be said about the life story of God's true Servant, one thing that the poetry of 2 Isaiah wants to make clear is that "he had done no violence [Hebrew *khamas*]" (Isa 53:9).

In the Reverence School narrative, the paradigm example of the destruction of social harmony through escalating violence occurred in the days of Noah, when God sent a flood to destroy the earth. With the waters of the Genesis flood, God temporarily eradicated all human irreverence and rivalry. These vices had defied God's creation-charge and corrupted human togetherness, creating a catastrophic crisis. The Reverence School narrative describes the crises as follows: "Now the earth was corrupt in God's sight, and the earth was filled with violence [Hebrew *khamas*]" (Gen 6:11 RS).

Abhorring violence and its power to corrupt human community, the Reverence School strand strongly advocates pacifism. At first, Genesis even proscribes killing animals and eating their meat. Before the flood, every human was a vegetarian, and every animal was herbivorous (see Gen 1:29–30; 9:2–3 RS; cf. Isa 65:25).

As far as interpersonal relations go, God's servant people are to shun envy and aggression. The Reverence School narrative even prefers not mentioning famous biblical quarrels. To cite two examples, it describes neither the strife between Abraham's and Lot's herders (Gen 13:6, 11b–12 RS) nor the rivalry of Jacob and Esau (Gen 26:34–35; 27:46–28:2 RS).

Homicide is particularly anathema in the Reverence School strand. Murder violates the status and role that God has assigned to human beings since the creation. It directly contradicts God's intentions and hopes for the world (Gen 9:6; cf. 1:26–27 RS).

Amazingly, despite that it must account both for Pharaoh's defeat and for the conquest of Canaan, the Reverence School depicts no wars or battles of Israel. At the exodus, the people's only role is to depart Egypt peaceably and "boldly," trusting in God's prerogative (Exod 14:8 RS). At the conquest of Canaan, they should have shown the same calm, pacifist attitude (Num 14).[10]

As in the poems of 2 Isaiah, the texts of the Reverence School illustrate how God has a special relationship with the peripheral and downtrodden. Note in particular how the laws of sacrifice in the Reverence School portions of Leviticus show a special love of the poor. The unique wording of Leviticus 4:31 suggests that the Lord is especially pleased with the sin offerings of common people from the countryside. Leviticus 5:6–13 makes the special provision that a poor person may offer two birds instead of a goat or a lamb. If even a few birds are beyond their means, the poorest of the poor can make a cereal offering. There is no doubt that God makes extraordinary concessions on behalf of the needy.[11]

God's special presence with the lowly is also clear from Israel's saving history. Perhaps most notably, God intervened for the exodus generation at the point where Egypt had really "made their lives bitter" (Exod 1:14 RS), where they were nearly paralyzed by a "broken spirit" (Exod 6:9 RS). As in 2 Isaiah, in the Reverence School narrative of Exodus the poor in spirit find themselves strangely blessed. They are the ones to experience God's "outstretched arm" and "mighty acts" (Exod 6:6; cf. Isa 40:10; 51:5; 53:1).

> See, the Lord GOD comes with might, and his arm rules for him; his reward is with him, and his recompense before him. —Isa 40:10

True servants of God even embrace willed suffering, according to the Reverence School. Bafflingly, it "was the will of the LORD" to put the Suffering Servant in harm's way, "to crush him with pain" (Isa 53:10). So too, God allowed Abraham and Sarah to struggle through years of infertility and childlessness before Isaac was born (Gen 11:30; 16:3; 17:17; 21:5 RS). Only after their bodies had withered and grown fully sterile did God intervene in wonder. When any possibility of self-sufficiency was gone, Sarah and Abraham miraculously began a rapidly multiplying family, and quickly forgot their earlier indignities (cf. Isa 51:1–3; 54:1).

Though they bore God's promise for years in anguished humiliation, Abraham and Sarah lived "blameless" all the while, and they ultimately found joy in the promise's fulfillment (Gen 17:1; 21:1).[12] God performed mightily in the end, exactly as promised. In a theology of reverence, calm and courageous servitude repeatedly becomes the means of God to break through impasses and light up the world. In the end, such servitude leads the humble to exaltation.

Ruminating on Isaiah 50:4–11

Let us turn to delve deeply into one of Isaiah's Servant Songs, specifically the third song found in Isaiah 50:4–11. The passage reads as follows:

> [4] The Lord GOD has given me /
>   the tongue of those who are learners, //
> that I may know how to sustain /
>   the weary with a word. //
> Morning by morning he wakens— /
>   wakens my ear /
>   to listen as those who are taught. //
> [5] The Lord GOD has opened my ear, /
>   and I was not rebellious, /
>   I did not turn backward. //
> [6] I gave my back to those who struck me, /
>   and my cheeks to those who pulled out the beard; //
> I did not hide my face /
>   from insult and spitting. //
>
> [7] The Lord GOD helps me; /
>   therefore I have not been disgraced; //
> therefore I have set my face like flint, /
>   and I know that I shall not be put to shame; /
>   [8] he who vindicates me is near. //
> Who will contend with me? /
>   Let us stand up together. //
> Who are my adversaries? /
>   Let them confront me. //

⁹ It is the Lord GOD who helps me; /
    who will declare me guilty? //
All of them will wear out like a garment; /
    the moth will eat them up. //

¹⁰ Who among you fear the LORD /
    and obey the voice of his Servant? //
When they walk in darkness /
    and have no light, //
let them trust in the name of the LORD /
    and rely upon their God. //
¹¹ But all of you who are kindlers of fire, /
    lighters of firebrands. //
Walk in the flame of your fire, /
    and among the brands that you have kindled! //
This is what you shall have from my hand: /
    you shall lie down in torment. //¹³

What better way is there to come to know the Suffering Servant than to read such a self-description? Fearlessly and transparently, the Servant depicts himself and his experience in his own words. Candidly revealing his characteristic intentions and actions, he illumines the core nature of biblical servanthood in its ideal form. Yet it will take a hearty effort to understand and digest what the Servant here sets before us. Rumination and reflection will be necessary, for the Servant's language is poetry, tantalizingly suggestive rather than crisply explicit.

What the Servant initially reveals is his studious devotion to his Lord, a trait we recognize from descriptions of royal servants in biblical literature. Just as royal servants are a king's confidants, committed to realizing his interests, so the Suffering Servant tunes his ear to his Lord's purpose and work. God daily opens his understanding to the divine will, a will centering on helping the suffering and afflicted.

The Servant's commitment to learn—his open, apprentice's ear (vv. 4–5)—is an initial sign of his extreme reverence. An intimate experience with *awe* would best explain his teachable spirit. Staring up steeply at the sheer height of that which rises far above humanity, the mind realizes its finitude, its necessary limits. The Holy dwarfs the mind and confronts a person with the realization that there will always be much to learn, no matter how expert at this or that a person may become. With repeat experiences of the Holy, a person learns how to open the ears and close the mouth, awaiting the disclosure of revelation.

God's revelation, according to verse 4, focuses on care of "the weary"—that is, the poor in spirit. God wants the Servant to speak fitting, timely words to the faint and broken. They are to occupy the Servant's full attention as he attends to the Lord God's will. Isaiah 40:31 refers to the same class of people, using the exact same Hebrew term ("be weary, faint"). It describes them as gaining true strength from God, which empowers them to mount up with wings like eagles.

If the Servant's goal in all his training is to attend skillfully to faint and weary people, he is a truly selfless individual. There is no political advantage or profit in helping those less fortunate than oneself, who have no wealth or standing. One does it purely out of a spirit of friendship, a spirit of reverence.

The heart of the reverent person warms with sympathy for her or his fellow human beings, no matter how lowly or impoverished they may be. Even the peripheral and downtrodden may share an equally fervent devotion to God's person and will, thus compelling our attention and respect. What is more, the reverent soul desires what company it can find in making its way forward in a vast, overwhelming world. It is self-defeating to exhaust oneself in isolation, relying only on one's horde of wormy, rotting manna.

Verses 5 and 6 of our passage show just how far God calls the Suffering Servant to pursue a radical lifestyle of service and other-centeredness. He must willingly suffer the attacks of many who oppose him, bearing not only their physical torments but also their acts of humiliation. He must stand there, taking their assaults. He must face them without flinching as they spit in his face. In short, he must calmly put himself in harm's way and drop all defenses on behalf of others—specifically the "weary."

The poem does not spell out the details of the Servant's strategic plan for uplifting the weary, but its fundamental basis is apparent. The Servant is to suffer what violence he must in standing up for God's cause. All the while, he must steadfastly refuse to fight back or retaliate against those bent on abusing him. In a word, he is to use nonviolent resistance to set things right. The commitment to nonviolence and pacifism of the Reverence School shines in the Servant's manner of life.

Replacing hostility for his opponents with respectful nonviolence, the Servant aims to disarm their aggression and unmask their blind pride. His goal is to guide them toward a conversion of the heart. That is why verse 8 shows him confronting and challenging his opponents, exposing the ultimate futility of their position and contrasting the powerful rightness of his alternative manner of life. Such commitment to sway one's enemies and win them over at the risk of one's own safety is startling. It represents self-sacrifice without limits.

Replacing hostility for his opponents with respectful nonviolence, the Servant aims to disarm their aggression and unmask their blind pride.

The Servant's manner of life is rare in our modern experience, but thankfully not without attestation. The dramatized role of the Servant in our poem has taken on flesh and blood at a variety of points in human history around the globe. He has appeared incarnate in India under Mahatma Gandhi's example, in the American South under Martin Luther King's leadership, and among Chinese students protesting peacefully against their government in Tiananmen Square. In each case, calm, courageous souls among the "weary" have risked stepping out, putting themselves forward as agents for justice and human transformation. They have been mentally and spiritually active and engaged, while determinedly eschewing not only physical violence but also any internal violence to their own spirits.

Refusing to add to the world's hostilities, they have put the brakes on the inevitable cycle of violence and revenge that ignorance, fear, and envy inevitably churn. Instead, by presenting themselves as vulnerable parties, exposing the neck and the underbelly, they have laid bare their opponents' selfishness and egoism. They have tried to awaken in them compassion for their fellow human beings made in God's image. Thus, they have planted the seeds of human rapprochement in the world.

To elaborate on another concrete example of a time when the lifestyle of Isaiah's Servant came to life, one day in 1943 in Berlin, the capital of the Third Reich, thousands of Jews with German wives joined the class of the "weary" when they found themselves arrested by the Gestapo. Simultaneously, their non-Jewish wives took up the role of servants of the Lord. On the day after their husbands' arrest, six thousand of the wives assembled at the makeshift prison in Berlin holding their loved ones. They disregarded the rebukes of the center's guards and deflected their efforts to disperse them. They paid no mind to the SS's machine guns, ignored the presence of Gestapo forces headquartered nearby. They simply massed in the square outside the detention center, called for their husbands, and demanded their release. Amazingly, the women's public, nonviolent resistance achieved its intended effect. The Gestapo proved willing to negotiate. Eventually, they released their captives.

The Servant's approach of frailty paradoxically lands him authority and freedom of choice. Rather than describing his enemies' initiative in his ordeal, the language of verse 6 surprisingly portrays the Servant as the primary orchestrator of his experience: he gives his back to those who would strike him; he offers his cheeks "to those who pulled out the beard"; he does not hide his face. His plan of action purposely entails suffering and degradation, and he voluntarily yields himself to his fate. The Servant is in full control of the situation in which he suffers. There is veritable majesty in the way he commands his emotions, spirit, and experience.

Nonviolent resistance can entail this very sort of paradoxical turning of the tables on claimants to power. It can force their hand, making them exercise their physical aggression at visible and awkward moments. Pushing them off the fence of conformity and passivity, it brings them up against their complicity in a cold and unjust world. Absent any veneer of propriety, will they carry through with their threats? Will they actually bully the helpless for all to see, paining their private consciences and arousing public indignation? Or, rather than proving themselves bullies and brutes, will they awaken to the humanity of their victims and rethink their position?

Equally striking is how thoroughly the Servant, even under attack, avoids bitterness and enmity. How tempting under the torturous circumstances of verse 6 to give oneself over to feelings of rage and revenge, yet the verse gives no hint of this. Rather, the Servant maintains the same spirit of patience, restraint, and meekness observable in other of Isaiah's Servant Songs. He remains blameless, just as Abraham and Sarah did for all those years of infertility (according to the RS narrative).

As in Isaiah 42:2, he does not "cry or lift up his voice, or make it heard in the street." Instead of leaning on indignation and anger to sustain him through his ordeal, he leans on the Lord God (50:7, 10), who ultimately vindicates his work (vv. 8–9).

I would argue that a capacity for awe—an appreciation for the reality of the Holy—sustains the Servant's calm, pacifist stance. Frustration and bitterness tend to melt quickly away before a swelling experience of God's transcendent mystery. As inarticulate awe mounts, one feels oneself increasingly without ego, without the ego's inevitable rebellion against personal injustices and injuries. A truly reverent person cannot help but let all else go in order to keep her or his ear open to heaven's guidance. His ear open to God, the Servant can follow no other course than unswerving obedience to his Lord despite persecution and suffering (v. 5).

> Frustration and bitterness tend to melt quickly away before a swelling experience of God's transcendent mystery.

All human beings, even oppressors, have embers of reverence within their souls, a capacity for experiencing awe before the holy. Nonviolent resistance can fan and awaken those glowing coals. By unveiling how oppressors necessarily diminish their own humanity, degrading themselves through a merciless and insulting spirit, such work of resistance aids them in feeling impoverishment and shame. To awaken shame, culpability, and profaneness is to stimulate reverence.

For nonviolent risk-taking to effectively awaken reverence, it needs two essential ingredients. First, the risk-taking agents must be innocent, undeserving of their punishment. Otherwise, their opponents can too easily turn them into scapegoats. No crisis is created for oppressors, and thus no opportunity for conversion, if they appear to be merely rendering the guilty their due.

Second, the mission must have lofty purpose, and not merely revolve around the risk-takers' own wants and needs. Much of the mission's power comes from its agents' depth of resolve, which allows them to stand firm for what they hold to transcend their own selves in value. Standing firm in their devotion, the agents for change create a crisis for their oppressors. They confront them with a model of self-transcendence that directly contradicts their self-satisfaction and complacency.

The suffering hero of Isaiah 50:4–11 meets both of these criteria. First, the Servant's sufferings are undeserved. His ear is awake to God, ready to obey God's word, as both verse 4 and verse 5 emphasize. By repeating the image of the open ear, the poetry drives home the Servant's unreserved submission to God's will. Second, the Servant, determined to carry out God's will, has set his face hard as flint in the direction of his mission (v. 7). He can honestly report that he has not drawn back from his God-appointed task, has never considered running away (v. 5). His fervor and resolve witness that something lofty inspires and directs him.

Indeed, the Servant claims God's direct support and immediate presence in his work. The Hebrew of verse 8 begins with the adjective "near," emphasizing that God is at hand in the Servant's obedience, humility, and suffering. God supports the selfless and the other-centered, because their stance toward existence takes its cue from God's very own playbook.

The poetry of verse 10 sets the two phrases "fear the LORD" and "obey . . . his servant" in synonymous parallelism. It asks the reader to equate obedience of God with submission to God's apprentice, the Suffering Servant. The equation is remarkable! It inextricably couples the work of God and the work of the Servant. Without a doubt, the will of the Servant reflects the will of the Lord. He and God are practically interchangeable, at least if we are to take the poetic parallelism of Isaiah 50:10 seriously. The Servant reveals God's playbook to the world. It is God's nature to hold nothing back, to abate nothing of God's own, but to give everything in love to the weary on earth.

Continuing the Conversation . . .

The best book on the identity of the Suffering Servant that I know of is David J. A. Clines, *I, He, We, and They: A Literary Approach to Isaiah 53,* Journal for the Study of the Old Testament Supplement Series 1 (Sheffield: JSOT Press, 1976). Nathaniel Hawthorne's story of the Great Stone Face is widely available. It is included, for example, in Nathaniel Hawthorne, *Hawthorne's Short Stories,* ed. N. Arvin (New York: Vintage, Knopf, 2005).

We have looked briefly at some key passages of the Reverence School's narrative in the book of Exodus. For further fine theological interpretations of these passages, I recommend Walter Brueggemann, "The Book of Exodus: Introduction, Commentary, and Reflections," in vol. 1 of *The New Interpreter's Bible,* ed. L. E. Keck (Nashville: Abingdon, 1994), 677–982.

On violence as a fundamental threat to community, see Gil Bailie, *Violence Unveiled: Humanity at the Crossroads* (New York: Crossroad, 1995).

CHAPTER FIVE

Atonement and Exuberance

Exuberance and power, 2 Isaiah teaches, are found most unexpectedly. We receive them as divine gifts, independent of payment or dessert. They are ours to enjoy, if only we claim God's mercy, calmly letting go of pride and anxiety. Wondrous spiritual invigoration is ours, if we direct our attention expectantly toward the Lord, taking on a *waiting* spirituality.

Across the centuries, the faithful have reported countless experiences of the invigoration that comes through waiting on God. In his classic exposition of 2 Isaiah, Henry Sloane Coffin cites several ready examples.[1] He notes how Sir Henry Stanley, the famed British explorer of Africa, wrote in his diary that his steady relationship with God "lifted me hopefully over the one thousand five hundred miles of Forest tracks, eager to face the day's perils and fatigues." In like manner, Coffin cites the example of John Wesley, the eminent, tireless spiritual leader and founder of Methodism. At age eighty-two, Wesley declared, "I do not know

Henry Sloane Coffin: one of the United States' most famous ministers, president of Union Theological Seminary in the City of New York, Yale University Trustee, and moderator of the Presbyterian Church USA (1877–1954).

what weariness means. I am never weary of writing or preaching or traveling, but am just as fresh at the end as at the beginning."

Let us, like Stanley and Wesley, rely firmly and steadily on God's prerogative in existence and empowerment for the work of ministry. Let us avail ourselves of the refreshment and strength that comes from repose in Isaiah's God, from waiting on the Holy One in a stance of servanthood.

But what does such a spiritual posture of repose really entail? What would it look like to be honest about its difficulties, about what it would take to really follow through with the commitment? I want to pose and reflect upon these questions in this chapter.

The costs of servanthood, according to 2 Isaiah, are not cheap. In order that we might find access to true spiritual force, our poems strongly advocate an abnegation of the self and a turning outward in other-centeredness. A lifestyle of servanthood, oriented toward God and our neighbors, 2 Isaiah proclaims, is the significant and necessary commitment to be made for growth in divine grace and ultimate exaltation.

Obviously, all thinking people will want to count this cost. It seems unreasonably arduous and painful! Humility and other-centeredness appear to be completely counterintuitive means to finding fulfillment and joy. Letting down our guard seems unsafe; loving the unlovable, oxymoronic. What sense is there in cultivating respect and friendship for subordinates, not to speak of weaklings and fools? Is it not a thankless and futile undertaking to pour oneself out for the multitudes, for the world's lost sheep? The need of the great mass of earth's souls is large indeed; it is deep—in fact, inexhaustible.

Even if we find ourselves able to affirm the paradoxical power of other-centered servanthood, how can we possibly break free from our ignorance and pride in order to take up our crosses? Where do we find the sufficiency and strength to overcome our innate self-concern and self-orientation?

All of us, from birth, crave safety and comfort. Treasuring success and getting ahead, we naturally focus on "our own way" (Isa 53:6). Is not what Isaiah is calling for a death-judgment on the self? Is not such a call something we can hardly bring ourselves to accept?

Such a self-judgment *is* unworkable and unacceptable, Reverence theology holds—unworkable, that is, absent an ever-mounting awe and devotion before a dawning of the Holy. God must reveal the "arm of the LORD," as promised in 2 Isaiah. Without a sense of wonder and the virtue of reverence we may labor to hand ourselves over to God, but will have little success. We will simply find ourselves too weak, too untrue.

Although we are powerless on our own to put aside our self-concern, God's rending advent, should we experience it, could smelt and refine our egos in the heat of burning holiness. Our egos purified and tested, we could then take on God's freely provided cover, sufficiency, and invigoration. Only then, free of egoism, safely covered, and newly empowered, might we commune with the Holy and serve God truly.

In his "Holy Sonnet 14," John Donne (1572–1631), a poetic genius among Anglican divines, captured well the cost of a full repose in God. He admits in the poem that he has labored without success at waiting on the Lord. As a result, using shocking language of divine violence, he prays for the Lord to forcefully overthrow his will.

Batter my heart, three-person'd God; for you
As yet but knock; breathe, shine, and seek to mend;
That I may rise, and stand, o'erthrow me, and bend
Your force, to break, blow, burn, and make me new.
I, like an usurp'd town, to another due,
Labour to admit you, but O, to no end.
Reason, your viceroy in me, me should defend,
But is captived, and proves weak or untrue.
Yet dearly I love you, and would be loved fain,
But am betroth'd unto your enemy;
Divorce me, untie, or break that knot again,
Take me to you, imprison me, for I,
Except you enthrall me, never shall be free,
Nor ever chaste, except you ravish me.[2]

The sonnet is highly controversial because of Donne's resort to being strong-armed by God. Donne implores God to use force, to "break, blow, burn, and make me new." "I, Except you enthrall me, never shall be free." Admittedly provocative and disturbing, Donne's language of violence is, nevertheless, true to the Scriptures. The ego does not surrender its possession of our lives without a hearty struggle. We will remain self-possessed unless the ego is painfully and decisively overwhelmed, brought down with a hard thud. Thus, the Scriptures speak positively of a heart that is "shattered," "broken," and "crushed" before God. Such a heart is the sacrifice most acceptable to the Holy One (Ps 51:17).

> The sacrifice acceptable to God is a broken spirit; a broken and contrite heart, O God, you will not despise.
> —Ps 51:17

The invaluable reward of God's servants is an ever-closer experience of God, yet this entails a species of violence. To increasingly feel the uncreated fire of divine otherness means more and more to be shorn and husked of one's disguises. That hurts! It is to discover all one's pretensions and airs being melted away like wax under a flame.

The Emphasis on Self-Sacrifice in the Reverence School

A wrenching sacrifice of self is part and parcel of a loving surrender to God, according to the Reverence School. God's servants Abraham and Sarah modeled a life of deep sacrifice, as we have seen. They steadfastly endured profound losses in life, confirming the strength of their servanthood. They trusted that by patiently waiting on God they would eventually receive God's best for them.

The Reverence School's emphasis on sacrifice included offering animals up for ritual slaughter at the Jerusalem temple. These ritual offerings, which were central to the school's spirituality, provided Israel with a sacral discipline for living into Abraham and Sarah's servant-oriented form of life. They were a temple-centered means of training in the practice of God-centeredness.

The public immolation of atoning sacrifices cannot be construed, in keeping with some common interpretations, as bribes or gifts to God. Any worshiper offering a sacrifice of atonement with the thought "I give, you give, O God" was sadly deluded. In the Reverence School Scriptures, the Holy One of Israel is self-dependent, noncontingent, already in full possession of all earth's life, and absolutely unwilling to accept any sort of human care or feeding.

Atoning sacrifices have nothing to offer God, nor do they satisfy or placate God, as if God were anthropomorphic.

To reinforce these points, the Reverence School Scriptures specify that sacrificial animals, when offered for atonement, are not to be consumed by fire so that their substance wafts heavenward. In contrast to procedures elsewhere in the Bible, their meat is to be eaten by the temple priests (Lev 6:26; 7:7; 14:13 RS). The Reverence School further differs from other biblical sources in avoiding any language of atoning sacrifices placating God through a soothing aroma (contrast, e.g., Gen 8:21 [J]; Lev 26:31 [HS]; Ezek 20:41).[3]

How then do we interpret animal sacrifice in the Reverence School Scriptures? I submit we must meet their scandal of violence head on, starting with the scandal of the immolation of animals. The gory violence of ancient animal sacrifices is shocking to us today, but it was gory and tragic in ancient times as well, even for the members of the Reverence School.

The writers of the Reverence School Scriptures recognized that animal victims were no mere possessions of their owners who offered them, but living beings capable of pain and anguish. They express explicit concern for the life of animals, which comes directly from God (Gen 9:4 RS). Humans dare not kill God's creatures frivolously, callously, or carelessly, they caution in their Scriptures. The ritual sacrifice of animals, therefore, is an intense, excruciating, and profound occasion in the thinking of the school. It is a moment of intimate contact with the amoral, inscrutable dimensions of divinity.

The animal death entailed in temple sacrifices pales before a greater offense, however. What is most shocking is to realize that the life required to be offered in these rites was fundamentally not that of the animal but of its owner. Our school of authors teaches that the animals offered at the temple by transgressors within Israel died in their owners' place, as their stand-ins.[4]

Within the Reverence School Scriptures, we must reckon with a call of God on the lives of God's servants. Drawing near before the Holy One means death—death to impurity, death to ego-centeredness. The meaning of rites of sacrifice turns on this crucial theological dictum.

Faced with the Holy, human life is forfeit, at least according to the Reverence School. Nadab and Abihu, approaching God presumptuously, died before the Lord in their neglect of divine otherness (Lev 10:2 RS). Later, Zimri and Cozbi, joined in sexual intercourse before Baal of Peor, similarly suffered death (Num 25:8 RS). In their demise, they became a propitiation for the sins of the people, a means of atonement for the entire camp.

Baal of Peor: the manifestation of Baal, the pagan fer-
tility deity, at a place named
Peor in the hills above the
eastern Jordan Valley.

The death-dealing power of the Holy is not all gloom and doom, however, as the above examples probably suggest. To view the lethal power of God's presence as entirely about judgment and propitiation would vastly underestimate the full dimensions of the Holy. Did not John Donne earnestly and expectantly pray for God to overthrow, smelt, and re-create his human soul? For him, laying down his life to let God's will be done was a positive and wondrous experience, desperately to be desired. He thought of God's deathblows as wielding *transformation,* not *termination.*

Impassioned lovers are intimately familiar with the profundity of Donne's thinking. They feel its truth in the *little death* they die as their lovemaking climaxes. (I am speaking of the passionate release that the French have termed *la petit mort.*) This "death" constitutes a positive and spiritual experience of submergence and release. Though a daring illustration, we have here an entrée for a positive appreciation of the death-wielding energy of the Holy.

For sinners to experience a spiritual release along the lines of the *little death* would be a true gift of God. Such a death must appeal to the true believer, as it represents a sweet deliverance from the sort of wrath borne by the couple Zimri and Cozbi, whom Phinehas had to kill. Indeed, it represents the sort of smelting and refining of the human ego for which Donne passionately longed in his sonnet.

I propose to bite the bullet and submit that the Reverence School devotes so much attention to animal sacrifices because it has discovered in them a wondrous little death, a miracle of human awakening and transformation. To this school's thinking, sacrifices of atonement entail self-transcendence. They evoke a spiritual death to selfishness and egoism and a rebirth before God. They are an answer to Donne's prayer.

Through their disquieting, bloody mystery, animal sacrifices evoked deep awe within worshipers, nurturing the virtue of reverence. As Israelite believers participated in sacrificial rites, they publicly and voluntarily reoriented their existence. Abandoning self-centeredness, they opened up space for the Holy One to be number one in their lives.

At least one common misconception about atonement, strongly argued for by Immanuel Kant (1724–1804), can now be immediately corrected. Against Kant, it need not necessarily be "irrational and immoral" for atonement to involve the idea of substitution. Although animals, not humans, are the ones to suffer literal death in atoning sacrifices, these rituals revolve around personal reformation and renewal, not escaping personal liability. They have nothing to do with disowning one's guilt, avoiding justice, or scapegoating another being.

> **Immanuel Kant:** a highly influential German philosopher oriented on the Enlightenment, who devoted considerable critical reflection to morality (1724–1804).

The Reverence School's rituals of atonement radiated *dissevering* power. That is, they severed worshipers' ties to their self-oriented world of competition and hording (major vices according to the Reverence School Scriptures: see their story about manna, treated in chapter 4). They freed up worshipers' inner beings for friendship and communion with God and with neighbor.

Unlike inanimate objects, sacrificial animals are sentient beings. They feel pain; they resemble and express the human self. In making their sacrifices, ancient worshipers were immolating that which expresses their being, that which embodies their sentience.[5] Their animal's death entailed a representative, *inclusive* place-taking (German: *Stellvertretung*). Part of them died with their animal, the part that oriented them to selfishness and greed.

Before the sacrificing of the animal, the worshiper would lay hands upon it (e.g., Lev 1:4; 4:29 RS). The gesture did not happen with all sacrifices, just with bloody ones that aimed at atonement. Thus, it was doubtless more than a mere signal of ownership. Through the gesture, worshipers identified their inner beings with the animal victims, incorporated themselves in the animals' imminent deaths.[6] A current between owner and animal came alive through intimate touch. As the animals died, the lives of their owners were vicariously poured out before God. This is the heart of ritual atonement for the Reverence School. This is participatory, dedicatory atonement worked out with a passion.

Anthropology offers several illuminating parallels, including Vedic, Muslim, and Nuer rites where sacrificial animals are specifically identified with the lives of their owners. The Nuer, a traditional cattle-raising people of the southern Sudan, rub ashes on the backs of their sacrificial victims. In this act, they are identifying themselves intimately with their animals, designating them to represent that part of themselves that they view as selfish and evil, in need of elimination. In addition to rubbing ashes on his offering, a Nuer elder once made clear the symbolism of his sacrifice by cutting off his finger and casting it away. His gesture of self-mutilation reinforced his intention to immolate a part of himself through his act of animal sacrifice. He was determined to cast off his old persona, to become a new being.

The Shilluk people, who are neighbors of the Nuer, offer further help in understanding the sacrificial symbolism of Leviticus. As he offered up an animal victim, the Shilluk king would publicly proclaim the animal's flesh and blood to be the same as his own. This explicit evidence of vicarious identification with one's animal sacrifice strongly supports the overall conclusion about sacrifice of E. E. Evans-Pritchard, the renowned social anthropologist: "What one consecrates and sacrifices is always oneself."[7]

E. E. Evans-Pritchard: a British social scientist at Oxford University who played a key role in the development of modern social anthropology (1902–1973).

Evans-Pritchard's assertion appears to me to represent a rather profound truth, which strongly reverberates with classic Christian understandings of the cost of genuine servanthood. The cost is nothing less than having a part of you cut away, freeing up space for God, taking on God's ideal ennoblement. An ancient Greek hymn of Christianity reads:

My God, shall sin its power maintain
And in my soul defiant live!
'Tis not enough that Thou forgive,
The cross must rise and self be slain.[8]

The hymn expresses something very like the theology of sacrifice of the Reverence School. It remains an enigma, of course, that God's cure for violence, the pandemic contagion destroying us all (Gen 6:11–13 RS), is nothing other than a species of violence, namely, self-sacrifice.

The theology of the Reverence School recognizes that people often find that remorse and contrition are not enough to deal with their guilt, to become reconciled with God.[9] Sinners often find they must go farther, take personal responsibility, and somehow make amends in order to find true freedom and peace. "Reparation" for affronts against God, according to Leviticus, may be accomplished by means of a particular atonement offering, a *reparation offering* (Hebrew *'asham*; NRSV *guilt offering*; see Lev 5:14–6:7 RS). As we shall see, this species of atonement becomes particularly important in the poetry of 2 Isaiah (see Isa 53:10).

A reparation offering is one of several types of sacrifices appropriate when an Israelite commits sin. Unlike the better-known *purification offering* (NRSV: "sin offering"), its purpose is not to cleanse the sanctuary of impurity. Rather, having realized their guilt, those who offer an *'asham* are setting things right, answering for wrongs, and bearing their consequences.[10]

It is highly appropriate—very fitting indeed—that the poetry of 2 Isaiah should zero in on the Reverence School's reparation offering as the sacrifice most needed by the exiles. The Isaiah school understood the exile to be the result of Israel's pride, sacrilege, and defection from God (Isa 1:4; 6:5; 59:2–3). They stressed the people's need to get clean, to purify themselves (Isa 1:18; 44:22; 52:11; 64:6). The *'asham* is the very sacrifice one offers when in such dire straits (Lev 5:17–19 RS) when one has offended against God's burning sanctity (Lev 5:15–16 RS). It is how the unclean, the proud, and the leprous find deliverance and ceremonial purity (Lev 14:12, 14, 21 RS).

In Babylonian exile, there was no temple precinct to cleanse through purification offerings. "Sin offerings" (NRSV) were of no practical value. There was, however, a company of exiles collapsed under God's anger (Isa 40:2; 42:25; 51:17), estranged from the Lord (Isa 49:14; 51:13), battered, and cowed (Isa 41:17; 42:22). The reparation offering, not the sin offering, is the perfect one to offer for this troubled scenario. It is the specific sacrifice that offers absolution and healing for people who feel trapped, tormented, and despondent.[11]

I have thus far been considering religious sacrifice in terms of dissevering power and reparation costs, but it is also about exuberance and empowerment. Rudolf Otto captures this truth in discussing his concept of *consecration* in preparation for communion with the Holy. Let me flag a few key aspects of this dimension of sacrifice.

Otto describes consecration as an experience of means of grace, which comes to one who approaches the sphere of the Holy through sacrificial ritual. Partaking of the atoning power of the ritual, the worshiper receives from that which is holy something of its own quality. Through sacrificial rites, God bestows special blessings and virtues, including, most valuably, a capacity for communion with God, God's self.

Ethnographers have often observed cross-culturally the power of sacrifices to consecrate those who offer them. For example, they report that worshipers in sacrificial rituals of Morocco take on a special *baraka,* that is, blessing or virtue. In sacrificing to the Holy, they find themselves adorned with blessing, covered with sanctity.[12] To distribute such blessings among all attendees of their Great Feast, one of the tribespeople regularly performs a special ritual. Wrapping himself in the raw, bloody hide of a sacrificed sheep, he systematically beats on each family's tent with a stick. As the tents are struck, every inhabitant receives *l-baraka del-'id,* the blessing of the feast.

In like manner, the Skidi Pawnee Native Americans of Kansas and Nebraska regarded the smoke of their sacrifices as full of blessing. As the smoke wafted to the Supreme Being, Ti-ra'-wa, the people would grasp at it and direct it over themselves and their children. They believed it to be full of power to give them physical health, military victory, and agricultural bounty.

Within biblical religion, the Scriptures of the Reverence School embrace the notion that ritual sacrifice consecrates God's worshipers. It allows God's servants to approach near before the Lord in safety (Lev 16:1 RS). As in 2 Isaiah (Isa 40:2, 5), God's glory is a weighty and consuming fire, potentially lethal to anyone it contacts. It should appear to Israel only in the wake of a thorough, transformative preparation.

Sacrifices are required, the Reverence School texts tell us, to make ready for any tangible epiphany of God. This becomes especially clear as tabernacle service is inaugurated in Leviticus 9 and God appears in acceptance and response (vv. 23–24). With God's approach imminent (Lev 9:4, 6 RS), Israel jumps to consecrate priests, congregation, and sacral precincts through sacrifices. As the sacrifices start to burn, the people gratefully receive a double blessing from Aaron and Moses (Lev 9:22–23 RS). As fiery effulgences of divine glory appear, they shout in joy and fall in awe (Lev 9:24 RS). Sacrifice has surely consecrated this people. It has granted them the capacity to experience surprising relief, joyful surrender, and ecstatic adoration as they commune with God's awful majesty.

Ruminating on Isaiah 52:13–53:12

In the preceding chapter, we encountered the ideal hero of 2 Isaiah's Servant Songs and learned a good deal about him. He is one who patiently bears the abuse of the violent in order to help those in need. His patient, willing suffering powerfully begins to set things right within human experience. The Servant is misunderstood, humiliated, and abused, but ultimately triumphs. He stands up for God's cause and employs God's tactics of selflessness and unconditional love, and God vindicates his mission and grants him success. The Servant's example and victory is a powerful model for us, as we too strive to live as God's servants.

Turning now to the fourth Servant Song, our understanding of the Servant of the Lord deepens immeasurably. We learn the profundity of his self-sacrifice, its singularity that goes beyond anything we will ever be called to replicate. We realize that although we can hope to be this figure's disciples, we will never be his equals. Ernest may have become just like the old man of the mountain, but we can never claim the Suffering Servant's unique role in the history of salvation. We may well drink the same challenging cup of sacrifice as he does, but not to the same momentous effect.

In the poem, we see something wondrous transpire. God accepts the Servant's suffering and death as a reparation offering, an 'asham for others, indeed, for us, the readers. He accomplishes a veritable work of atonement, of expiation. In his unique experience, people come to recognize their guilt and alienation and see them put to an end. He is the ultimate, inimitable answer to Donne's prayer for God's will to triumph over the human self.

Did our song's authors expect to see the poetic persona of the Servant ever appear on earth in the flesh? Was their poem more than merely a theoretical meditation on discipleship? In a word, was it also a prophecy? If so, they were surely clueless as to how and where an incarnation of the Servant could ever come about. God's vision, visited upon them, was mystifying. Certainly, they would have been distressed to hear that it would take five hundred years for God's ideal Servant to finally appear among earth's masses. Yet, after just about that many centuries, when Jesus of Nazareth's life and death took shape, his followers found themselves drawn back to our poem. They came quickly to recognize in Jesus the perfect instantiation within history of the hero of Isaiah's Servant Songs.

52[13] See, my servant shall prosper; /
    he shall be exalted and lifted up, /
    and shall be very high. //
[14] Just as there were many who were astonished at him /
    —so marred was his appearance, beyond human semblance, /
    and his form beyond that of mortals— //
[15] so he shall startle many nations; /
    kings shall shut their mouths because of him; //
for that which had not been told them they shall see, /
    and that which they had not heard they shall contemplate. //

53[1] Who has believed what we have heard? /
    And to whom has the arm of the LORD been revealed? //
[2] For he grew up before him like a young plant, /
    and like a root out of dry ground; //
he had no form or majesty that we should look at him, /
    nothing in his appearance that we should desire him. //
[3] He was despised and rejected by others; /
    a man of suffering and acquainted with infirmity; //
and as one from whom others hide their faces /
    he was despised, and we held him of no account. //

[4] Surely he has borne our infirmities /
    and carried our diseases; //
yet we accounted him stricken, /
    struck down by God, and afflicted. //
[5] But he was wounded for our transgressions, /
    crushed for our iniquities; //

upon him was the punishment that made us whole, /
    and by his bruises we are healed. //
⁶ All we like sheep have gone astray; /
    we have all turned to our own way, //
and the LORD has laid on him /
    the iniquity of us all. //

⁷ He was oppressed, and he was afflicted, /
    yet he did not open his mouth; //
like a lamb that is led to the slaughter, /
    and like a sheep that before its shearers is silent, /
    so he did not open his mouth. //
⁸ By a perversion of justice he was taken away. /
    Who could have imagined his future? //
For he was cut off from the land of the living, /
    stricken for the transgression of my people. //
⁹ They made his grave with the wicked /
    and his tomb with the rich, //
although he had done no violence, /
    and there was no deceit in his mouth. //

¹⁰ Yet it was the will of the LORD to crush him with pain. //
When you make his life an offering for sin, /
    he shall see his offspring, and shall prolong his days; //
through him the will of the LORD shall prosper. /
    ¹¹ Out of his anguish he shall see light; //
he shall find satisfaction through his knowledge. /
    The righteous one, my servant, shall make many righteous, /
    and he shall bear their iniquities. //
¹² Therefore I will allot him a portion with the great, /
    and he shall divide the spoil with the strong; //
because he poured out himself to death, /
    and was numbered with the transgressors; //
yet he bore the sin of many, /
    and made intercession for the transgressors. //

Familiar traits of the Servant sound throughout the poem. His frailty, devotion, and nonviolence are starkly apparent. So is his orientation toward the weary, those who are disoriented and burdened.

We see him affording them harmony and well-being (*shalom*); "by his bruises," the poem's chorus confesses, "we are healed" (53:5).

This is the Servant we have come to know, and yet he surprises us anew. God has in mind to crush him. Because his anguish is redemptive, it opens up a safe and joyous approach to the Holy. Stunningly, it serves to "make many righteous" (53:10–11), forging a great interconnection between God in heaven and humanity on earth. Without a doubt, the Servant's suffering and death is the "arm of the LORD" (53:1), the dawning of the Holy. His work is God's self-revelation, smelting and remaking all things, for which Donne and all the rest of us wait (cf. 51:5; 52:10).

What is going on? Why would a faithful God want a devoted servant crushed with pain? How can our poem make such transcendent claims about the Servant's suffering and death?

The search for answers begins with the mysterious, freeing blessings experienced by the witnesses of the Servant's ordeal. Onlookers discover a heroic deliverer who willingly lays down his life on their behalf (53:5). His self-sacrifice uplifts them, even those bent on dealing him deadly harm, those who hate him (cf. Isa 50:6).

This is love at its pinnacle, radical love—love that is freely, unconditionally bestowed. Upheld by such love, one's need for guardedness and self-promotion vanishes. Such love lays a foundation for opening up to others, for self-transformation. With this kind of love in the world, one can let down one's defenses; one can relinquish one's self-concern. Drawn into a circle of shared, self-sacrificing love by the Servant, one is pushed to turn outward in friendship, love, and intimacy. The focus on "our own way" of Isaiah 53:6, which had previously characterized the lifestyle of the poem's witnesses, vanishes. Other-centeredness takes its place.

> With this kind of love in the world, one can let down one's defenses; one can relinquish one's self-concern.

What can be the Servant's motivation to make this gift of shared community to strangers and enemies? I believe he feels he has no choice but to reach out to those around him. He is so in touch with the reality of divine "overpoweringness" that he knows it cannot belong to one single self alone. To actually be in communion with the Holy is to discover that it must inevitably burst beyond your individual person. Eventually, it must claim the allegiance of all humanity, all creation.

The Servant certainly blesses the world with the makings of true human community, but he does more. Much more. He connects us closely to God as well as to our neighbors. His work and mission are thoroughly God-pointing, God-revealing. One senses this immediately in the Servant's dramatic otherness, his eerie numinousness. The Servant's suffering startles and dumbfounds those who witness it, leaving them with jaws dropped, speechless. "He shall startle many nations; kings shall shut their mouths because of him" (Isa 52:15a).

Onlookers to the Servant's ordeal come to perceive that which does not fit in with their regular patterns of experience and thought. "That which had not been told them they shall see, and that which they had not heard they shall contemplate" (Isa 52:15b). This feels like an experience of transcendence, an encounter with the Holy.

Readers of Hebrew have long been amazed at Isaiah 53:5, "He was wounded for our transgressions, crushed for our iniquities." The sounds of the original language echo eerily and mysteriously: sounds of *u-u-u, u-u-u.* Clearly, our poem's authors chose their Hebrew words carefully so readers would hear this uncanny sound and feel an utter awe.

The work of Rudolf Otto helps us account for the aura of otherness surrounding the Servant's person and work. Otto has shown that intense earthly humility, like that of the Servant, is exactly the flip side or "shadow" of God's heavenly glory. It is divine glory's "subjective reflection." The submergence of the Servant's ego, his willing sacrifice of his life, is the height of humility. It should not surprise us that such humility acts as a flawless mirror of God, truly reflecting divine overpoweringness and mystery.

As the Servant's trial proceeds, its witnesses discover calm, nonresistant endurance (53:7). They observe a purposeful, determined relinquishing of innocent life (53:10). The Servant "poured out himself to death" (53:12). Totally devoted to the divine beyond, carrying out God's purposes alone, the Servant acts in the absence of all natural drives, profit motives, and worldly support structures.

It is purely from God to lay down one's life on behalf of one's enemies, to give up one's self with no possibility of profit, advantage, or security. It is to knock away all struts and supports and to act from the Holy One in the midst of the self. Only one conclusion is possible. God is palpably present in the Servant's death.

Fascinatingly, anthropologists and ethnographers have observed that a similar amazement and awe often accompany sacrificial acts across many human cultures. Often, those offering ritual sacrifices perceive that their offerings somehow participate in the sanctity of transcendent holiness.

The traditional Kandhs people of Orissa, East India, held beliefs about the nature of their human sacrifices that form a case in point.[13] They offered such sacrifices, termed *Meriahs*, in past eras to the Earth goddess, Tari Pennu (or Bera Pennu). Fascinatingly, they regarded their victims as far more than commodities, dispensable for placating the Earth goddess. Far from treating them as mere castoffs, they honored them with an extraordinary reverence, bordering on adoration. Indeed, they treated them as somehow supernatural.

The natives' reverence for Meriahs was so prominent, in fact, that it confused the celebrated anthropologist James G. Frazer (1854–1941). Frazer wrongly supposed that since the Meriah possessed so much sovereign virtue, he must have been the Earth deity incarnate. After all, the Kandhs villagers prized every lock of hair and drop of spit they could collect from the Meriah before his sacrifice.

Frazer's younger contemporary, the anthropologist Edward A. Westermarck, called him on his premature conclusions. "A sacrifice is very commonly believed to be endowed with such a power," Westermarck countered. "[It appears] not as an original quality [of the sacrificial victim], but in consequence of its contact or communion with the supernatural being to which it is offered."[14]

Obviously, Isaiah's Suffering Servant bears some distinct resemblances to the Meriahs sacrificed by the Kandhs people. This prompts the question whether the Servant's death is somehow to be understood as a ritual sacrifice, an immolated offering like a Meriah. I believe the answer to this question to be *yes*. Several facets of our poem encourage this line of interpretation.

The Suffering Servant is without blemish (Isa 53:9b), a requirement of sacrificial offerings (e.g.,

Edward A. Westermarck: a Scandinavian social scientist who became a founder of academic sociology in Britain (1862–1939).

Lev 5:15 RS). He is likened to a lamb, slaughtered in the temple's courts (Isa 53:7). Like such a sacrifice, he bears the sin of many (53:12)—a technical idiom, the fixed language of ritual sacrifice (cf. Exod 28:38; Lev 10:17; 16:22 RS). Above all, we have the datum of Isaiah 53:10, which specifically equates the Servant with the *'asham;* it literally terms him a reparation offering. Though interpreters commonly resist the evidence, there is no mistaking its force. Our poem is presenting the Servant as an immolated offering to God. We are forced to conclude that he plays the part of a sacrifice for sin—perhaps the ultimate such sacrifice. How do we come to terms with this?

I submit that ceremonial and sacrificial language bubbles up in our poem precisely because the Servant's trial manifests the raw power of an immolated offering. His ordeal offers reparation to God and transforms the human spirit. What the Servant does for us fulfills the deepest hopes of the Reverence School for their sacrificial system. That is why our poets liken him to a sacrificial lamb. Like sacrifices of atonement at the temple, the Servant's death lets no one off the hook. Rather, it empowers people to recognize their brokenness and take responsibility for it. Those who begin to realize its significance are drawn into the heart of the victim's experience, becoming forever changed by his deed of love.

Numinousness looms large before those who witness the Servant's work, as we have seen. Holy otherness crests and washes over them as he dies. In the presence of the Holy, one becomes aware of one's profanity and scrambles for cover. In the presence of that which dwarfs the ego, one abandons selfishness and awakens to a larger vision of existence. The initial reaction of those who observe the Servant's appearance and manner reveals them to be lost and blind, sick and broken. Their dismissal of him as an embarrassing loser with nothing to offer shows them imprisoned by egocentricity, guilt, and fear (53:3).

As the Servant makes his sacrifice, however, the chorus of witnesses discovers their mistake and begins a new journey of healing. Starting with verse 4, the "we" of the poem realize that the Servant's sufferings are representative and *inclusive.* They are all about them and their rebirth. Amazingly, they realize, God's righteous Servant is putting himself in their position, taking their experience on his shoulders. Although the rank and status of a transgressor is foreign to him, he embraces it. He allows himself to get "counted among the wicked" (v. 12 NAB), "numbered among the sinners" (NJPS). He self-identifies with the chorus of the poem.

Their narcissistic world has been upside down, their impression of the Servant completely mistaken. The Servant is fully innocent, undeserving of any punishment (v. 9). He is quintessentially the "righteous one" of God (v. 11). This has startling implications for them. The suffering and infirmity that they despised in this man (v. 3) constitute their own infirmity and suffering (v. 4). He has inter-linked his soul with their souls, establishing an electric intimacy. The poetry reveals it deftly, repeating verse 3's key words in reverse order in verse 4, repeatedly juxtaposing "he/him" and "we/our" in verse 5. Specifically, the Suffering Servant is taking up the most hurtful part of themselves in order to break it away from them. In so doing, he grants them healing (v. 5). So that they can start living *right,* he bears their iniquities (vv. 11–12).

The Hebrew word order of verse 11 is emphatic. It is *their* iniqui-ties that the Servant takes on himself. It is a foreign state of alien-ation from God that he assumes, shares, and overcomes. This is precisely the function of atonement sacrifices at the temple. To bor-row from a saying of Nietzsche, they treat the human being not as an *individual* monad but as a *divisible* being—not as an *individuum* but as a *dividuum.* In an atonement offering, the selfishness and brutality in the human soul is cut away. It is cast off as surely as that Nuer elder, referenced above, chopped off a finger from his hand.

Friedrich Nietzsche: a widely read German philosopher, fond of aphorisms, who wrote influential critiques of religion, morality, and culture (1844–1900).

We can see in our poem how the chorus experi-ences the Servant's sacrifice as a death-judgment for the cold, dark aspects of their own inner selves. As they realize that the weaknesses and sufferings the Servant bears are theirs, not his own (53:4), their narcissism dies. They begin to care about the fate of someone they previously considered worthless scum.

As he gives up his life, the Servant's ordeal accomplishes a great conversion in the chorus, a great smelting and refining. Those who come to embrace the Servant's sacrifice leave behind their existence as judgmental scoffers and emerge from their narcissistic cocoons as frail, self-convicted human beings (53:5–6). The chorus admits they have wandered off, gotten lost in life. What is worse, their ignorance and selfishness has ripped, torn, and crushed a humble, innocent person. They mourn their responsibility for the torture of one who had nothing but love for them.

Our poem is not only about guilt and conversion, however, but also about the granting of joy. Across the cultures of the world, ritual sacrifices are often occasions of grace and blessing for those who participate in them. In the case of the East Indian Meriah offerings, worshipers believed their victims' flesh and ashes were imbued with intrinsic power to bless the land. They buried or scattered these remains in their fields to ensure good crops.

That is not all. They held the tears of the Meriah to have rainmaking power. His blood was the key to the local turmeric herb's redness. Even strands of the Meriah's hair or drops of his spittle, they believed, could bring blessing to a household. Villagers would beg for such samples in the period before his death.

The sacrifice of the Servant of the Lord has no less power than its anthropological parallels to radiate consecration and empowerment. The Servant's death tolls the end of sin and brokenness but also rings in new life. As Isaiah 53:5 makes clear, it draws the chorus of witnesses into a shared, harmonious mutuality with God and with other human beings—into "peace" (NIV; Hebrew *shalom*). The witnesses receive the same spirit of reconciliation that King Cyrus experienced, when he felt his ego die before the immensity of forces beyond his control (see chapter 1).

A mature, fully expanded form of the openness and vulnerability that arose between Cyrus and Croesus constitutes salvation, the promised reign of God. The sacrificial death of Isaiah's Servant of the Lord affords the very means of grace to attain this ideal. It carries away the sin of the many, in order that people may dwell in unity and come before God's presence as God's own children.

Ruminating on Isaiah 40:27–31

The sacrifice of the Suffering Servant opens up a channel of divine power for all of us. It empowers us to let go of our fear and envy, and turn outward in other-centeredness. It is God's provision, 2 Isaiah proclaims, to enable us to take up a lifestyle of servanthood ourselves, oriented on God and our neighbors. With this means of consecration available to us, we have the key to growth in divine grace. We have the secret of spiritual vitality and ultimate exaltation. As Isaiah 40, to which we now turn, puts it, we have the means to "mount up with wings like eagles" (v. 31).

Isaiah 40:27–31 showcases a joyful, exuberant reverence. It pictures God's people enveloped with power, youthfulness, and blessing. Nourished by exposure to the Holy, their souls take wing. This is the birthright of everyone reborn before God, renewed before pure, divine transcendence.

> ²⁷ Why do you say, O Jacob, /
>   and speak, O Israel, //
> "My way is hidden from the LORD, /
>   and my right is disregarded by my God"? //
> ²⁸ Have you not known? /
>   Have you not heard? //
> The LORD is the everlasting God, /
>   the Creator of the ends of the earth. //
> He does not faint or grow weary; /
>   his understanding is unsearchable. //
> ²⁹ He gives power to the faint, /
>   and strengthens the powerless. //
> ³⁰ Even youths will faint and be weary, /
>   and the young will fall exhausted; //
> ³¹ but those who wait for the LORD shall renew their strength, /
>   they shall mount up with wings like eagles, //
> they shall run and not be weary, /
>   they shall walk and not faint. //

Having shed their old selves, God's servants lay aside their weighty despair, fear, and profanity. In John Donne's language, they rise and stand, chaste and free. Unburdened, they emerge from their insular cocoons into a special relationship with divinity. They wake up and put their faces in the sunlight. They begin a new life, reveling in the warmth and renewal of streaming God-light, God-energy.

On earth, energy inevitably dissipates, entropy invariably increases. But the self-existent God, who stands apart from creation (v. 28), is unconstrained by our natural laws of thermodynamics. We need never doubt that God can and will act to bring blessing to creation and to the human community. Inscrutable, "unsearchable," God may not perform according to our sense of urgency or propriety, but God will perform.

Verse 31 takes us through a fourfold progression, as spiritual power wells up within the restored human soul. First, the soul receives fresh strength, replacing its old, insufficient power. Next, with new, God-given plumes, it spreads its wings. At last, pumped and primed, it sprints off in a blur of speed. Advancing forward, assured of success, the soul steadily eases into a confident, tireless stride. The final movement from a run to a walk is not retrogression. It is the power of God infusing the dailiness of existence. The verb "walk" in Hebrew can be a figurative expression for living one's life. If the exuberance of the Holy pervades such a walk, then it is no temporary state of ecstasy but a total life experience.

God's incommensurable glory is drawing near, 2 Isaiah proclaims; it is becoming accessible on earth. More than this, God's servants are actually beginning to participate in divine qualities, taking on attributes of the Holy One. Invigorated through the power of the "Creator of the ends of the earth," they are becoming God's intimates, born from above, interconnected with heaven.

Note the rhetorical repetition of identical verbs in the poetry. God "does not faint or grow weary" (v. 28). So also, God's people shall "not be weary," shall "not faint" (v. 31). They receive God's own strength, which God alone wields. What a possibility! With such strength, God controls the stars of heaven, leads out their host one by one (40:26). Such power is symphonic, tympanic, resounding with majesty.

This is quite a paradox, isn't it? We are by now familiar with reverence as a sobering virtue. We know that it means accepting human limitations, coming to terms with our finitude, brokenness, and mortality. Yet, our poem makes plain that sober reverence has a gleeful cousin. In its gleeful form, reverence washes over us, bathing us in divine strength and splendor (cf. Isa 46:13). It suffuses us with the hope and courage of a Henry Stanley, the fresh energy of a John Wesley.

The joyful reverence of our poem corresponds to that aspect of the knowledge of the Holy that Rudolf Otto termed the *overabounding*.[15] Otto astutely observed that religious awe before the numinous commonly entails a strange and mighty propulsion, a nonrational exuberance, a second birth. The rushing spirit of God wafts the ransomed soul upward, brings about a resurrection within the heart. Given its wings, the soul thrills in inexpressible vitality.

In his work the *Phaedrus,* Plato gives us a neat glimpse of this sort of spiritual dynamism making its epiphany. He describes a man beholding someone of sublime beauty, thereby momentarily glimpsing divine sublimity. Weakness and pain overtake the fellow on the spot. He quickly feels exposed, imperiled, and finally overpowered. Paradoxically, he is simultaneously filled with energy, with propulsion.

In her deeply insightful book *On Beauty and Being Just,* Elaine Scarry uses this very example to illustrate how an uncanny power flows from reverence, from self-abnegation: "Feathers are beginning to emerge out of [this fellow's] back, appearing all along the edges of his shoulder blades. Because this plumage begins to lift him off the ground a few inches, he catches glimpses of the immortal realm."[16] This unexpected, levitating energy, Scarry insists, is more than mere euphoria. To let go of the ego and encounter the sublime is to be propelled into a just and creative form of life.

Several centuries after Plato, the Greek critic Longinus echoed the insights of the *Phaedrus.* He wrote, "You see, by true sublimity our soul somehow is both lifted up and—taking on a kind of exultant resemblance—filled with delight and great glory, as if our soul itself had created what it just heard."[17] For Longinus, as the humble of spirit immerse themselves in true sublimity they actually feel the influx of divine power.

Saint Catherine of Genoa (1447–1510) had this to say about receiving God's overabounding power:

> I am bringing on my justice, it is not far off, my salvation shall not tarry; I will put salvation within Zion, and give to Israel my glory. —Isa 46:13 NAB

> Religious awe before the numinous commonly entails a strange and mighty propulsion.

> Plato: a classical Greek philosopher, who helped lay the philosophical foundations of Western culture (ca. 424–348 BCE).

The mouth is filled with burning sighs and amorous conceits, which rise from the heart, and seem ready to break forth in words powerful enough to break a heart of stone. But they find no utterance; the true and loving colloquy is going on within, and its sweetness cannot be conceived. The heart is made the tabernacle of God, into which, by himself and also by others, many graces are infused, which bear in secret wondrous fruits. This creature has a heaven within herself. (*Spiritual Dialogues*, Third Part, ch. 10)

By all means, we ought to access this power, avail ourselves of this infusion of blessing. God's bright glory is dawning upon us, and our souls by nature want to bask in it. As in the fourth Servant Song, however, we should not assume that this is automatic. Not everyone who witnesses a divine intervention is able to appropriate it.

It is to the poets, the "we" of Isaiah 53, that the arm of the Lord has been revealed (Isa 53:1). They labor diligently at their poetic artistry, because they want the rest of us, including all future readers of the song, to come to understand the Suffering Servant as they do. They want us to submit to God's new, creative redemption, to gain real life as God's trusting, expectant servants—progeny of the Suffering Servant. All of us are in need of this new life, of God's over-abounding power.

According to Isaiah 40:30, this includes even fresh youths and choice young men. To avoid eventual collapse, even the most robust and vigorous among us must tap into divine reality. To do so means to "wait for the LORD," to let God take us by the hand (v. 31). The Hebrew verb is *qawah*, "hope in faith," "look forward in eager anticipation."

To "wait for the LORD" (*qawah*) is to courageously stay with God. It is to live in dependence on the Lord, assured of God's power and understanding. Those who wait on the Lord expect that God will make things right at God's right time, and so take heart. Their prayer reflects confident watchfulness: "In you, Lord, is our hope; And we shall never hope in vain" (Episcopal *Book of Common Prayer*, 98).

Those who "wait" on God confess that they are spiritually "faint," ultimately "powerless" (v. 29). God is their best and only prayer, and they know it. Again, 2 Isaiah brings us back to that core paradox of reverence theology. The only sure way to tap into true power and success is to recognize one's human frailty.

As we respond existentially to the revealed holiness of God, we daily dethrone pride and the self. We increasingly allow God to circumscribe the self, to give it its proper boundaries. Appropriately bounded, the soul is freed for energetic participation and interaction with God and God's servants. It is ready to join the great spiritual dance, in which God's human collaborators move in perfect rhythm to the power-filled beat of heaven.

The power of the dance of servanthood is the power of synergy. God's dancers throb with being, vigor, and joy. They give themselves up to the dance, freely receiving God's divine gifts and freely offering back, in cyclic interchange, obedient love and ecstatic adoration.

Continuing the Conversation . . .

Henry Sloane Coffin's classic exposition of 2 Isaiah is well worth reading: "The Book of Isaiah, Chapters 40–66: Exposition," in *The Interpreter's Bible*, ed. G. A. Buttrick (Nashville: Abingdon, 1956), 5:419–773.

For strong arguments that Jesus identified with the ideal protagonist of Isaiah's Servant Songs, see Stephen L. Cook, *The Apocalyptic Literature*, Interpreting Biblical Texts (Nashville: Abingdon, 2003), 148–67.

The modern theological debate about the influence of Isaiah's fourth Servant Song on Jesus' ministry is well represented in the gripping essays collected in W. Bellinger Jr. and W. R. Farmer, eds., *Jesus and the Suffering Servant: Isaiah 53 and Christian Origins* (Harrisburg: Trinity Press International, 1998). To delve even more deeply into current scholarly debates on this topic, I recommend reading the newly translated volume edited by Bernd Janowski and Peter Stuhlmacher, *The Suffering Servant: Isaiah 53 in Jewish and Christian Sources*, trans. D. Bailey (Grand Rapids: Eerdmans, 2004).

CHAPTER SIX

The Majesty of Servanthood

Consider the simple word *majesty* and the variety of reactions it may provoke within you. Perhaps, in the mere word itself, you can detect a faint trace of divine otherness—of numinousness. This, at least, is the claim of Rudolf Otto in his classic study of the Holy. Sometimes in human experiences with majesty, Otto believes, we get an indirect glimpse of supernatural holiness.

Given the link between holiness and majesty, it is no surprise that the idea of majesty abounds in 2 Isaiah's texts. In our prophetic poems, God reigns atop the cosmos, "above the circle of the earth." Neither people nor any of their objects of preoccupation can rise to this level. To come before God's presence is to fall prostrate before a monarch like none other, immediately to experience a shrinking of the self. Compared to God, earth's inhabitants are "grasshoppers" (Isa 40:22; cf. 51:12).

Someday soon, every knee on earth will bow to the Lord, and every tongue swear allegiance (Isa 45:23; cf. 51:5; 52:7). Yet, for now, God reigns in stark otherness. Divine majesty is largely unknown and inaccessible to God's creation, which has abandoned the holy, the utterly *other*, in favor of service to idols (Isa 44:9–20).

Reaching out from the beyond, however, God has granted glimpses of divine majesty to one select people, Israel. According to the biblical story, Israel knows God's identity, having experienced God as their royal sovereign. They should never forget the fact, as God plainly requires when reminding them, "I am the LORD, your Holy One, the Creator of Israel, *your King*" (Isa 43:15, emphasis added). Indeed, they should be instrumental in revealing God's majesty on earth. If and when they show forth God's glory, earth's nations will come to know God truly (Isa 43:10; 44:5; 45:14; 49:7; 55:3–5; 60:1–3).

Israel's divine king plays second fiddle to no other being. "My glory I will not give to another," God proclaims (Isa 48:11; cf. Exod 7:12; 9:11 RS). Yet, our texts claim that God may choose to share royal glory, to put it on display in God's people. Israel, though dwelling far beneath God's royal throne room, may partake of heavenly majesty in order to accomplish God's purposes.

> My glory I will not give to another. —Isa 48:11

God's plan is to impart divine majesty to people in order to channel blessing to earth. Israel is to be God's regent in the world, God's royal vicar through whom God will shine. Displaying God's splendor, Isaiah prophesies, Israel will attract earth's nations, which will gather to bask in God's royal beauty. As all peoples assemble in response to Israel's beckoning, God's salvation becomes global (Isa 44:23; 49:3; 61:3).

According to our poems, God initiates this plan for global salvation in a startling, paradoxical manner. God's unlikely instrument is the Suffering Servant, whom we have been studying. In his sacrifice, divine majesty bursts upon earth as a surprise shaft of light from heaven. In him, God reveals God's ideal vicar, the true Israel of God's own heart. The Servant of the Lord is none other than the ideal earthly image of heaven's divine king.

Ruminating on Isaiah 52:13–15

Let us return briefly to Isaiah 52:13–15, the initial part of the fourth Servant Song that we have already surveyed. The song bountifully repays renewed meditation. Within the poem's opening strophe, we see Isaiah's Servant emerge with royal dimensions. As the section begins, God is telling us about the Servant's royal destiny.

¹³ See, my servant shall prosper; /
   he shall be exalted and lifted up, /
   and shall be very high. //
¹⁴ Just as there were many who were astonished at him /
   —so marred was his appearance, beyond human semblance, /
   and his form beyond that of mortals— //
¹⁵ so he shall startle many nations; /
   kings shall shut their mouths because of him; //
for that which had not been told them they shall see, /
   and that which they had not heard they shall contemplate. //

The verses open the song by declaring the great significance of the Servant. "See!" the poem begins; the Servant is more than meets the eye. Before him nations are startled, astonished even; their rulers are awestruck. This is no ordinary Israelite. He is God's true instrument, a manifestation of the Holy, an unveiling of God's mighty arm.

The Servant will surely "prosper," according to verse 13. He will certainly stare humiliation and death in the face, enduring their full brunt, but he will not go down the tubes. Rather, he will faithfully complete his mission of love, and in the end, God will vindicate his sacrificial life. Extravagant rewards will be his highest honors (53:12). It will all come about because of his insight into how to live life right. He gets it: the only life worth living is the life of reverence.

The Servant will do more than "prosper" as a commoner might. His success is regal in nature, akin to that of the ideal Davidic monarch of Isaiah 11. According to Isaiah 11, it is the messianic "branch of Jesse" who prospers, who achieves success through God-given wisdom and perception (Isa 11:2).[1] It is he who has deep "knowledge" (Isa 11:2; 53:11). He—Israel's ideal king—stirs the world's imagination, as the Servant does (Isa 11:10; 52:15). He, like the Servant, appears on earth's stage as a tender green plant, a young sapling (Isa 11:1, 8; 53:2).

> A shoot shall come out from the stump of Jesse, and a branch shall grow out of his roots. —Isa 11:1

We must not stop even at this, even at seeing the Servant as a triumphant, messianic ruler. He is destined for more, as the specific language of verse 13 pushes us to realize. Its phraseology is extremely suggestive; indeed, it is *allusive*—intertextual. Echoes of Scripture swell the verse with significance, pointing us back to an earlier vision of Isaiah, the vision of Isaiah 6 and the prophet's translation to God's heavenly throne room.

We looked at the temple vision of Isaiah 6 in chapter 1. We saw how the prophet peered into God's cloud of unknowing, heard the seraphs cry, "Yahweh is other! other! other!" and became filled with fascination and dread. Verse 1 of the chapter introduces God enthroned in glory, cloaked in awesome majesty. Its words grope to convey the experience. It is these very words that reappear in Isaiah 52:13, applied to God's Servant.

In Isaiah 6:1, recalling his commissioning, Isaiah states, "I saw the Lord sitting on a throne, *high and lofty* (Hebrew *rum* + *nasa'*). Isaiah 33:10 and 57:15 use the word pair as well, again with direct reference to God. It is amazing to hear these words now applied to our suffering hero. After stating that the Servant shall "prosper," 52:13 goes on to declare, "He shall be exalted and lifted up, and shall be very high," thus plainly applying attributes of the Holy One to the Servant of the Lord. Given this fact, we must connect the Servant's destiny with the majesty of the Holy. We must fall silent, contemplating his future aglow with transcendent, otherworldly glory.

Consider the ramifications of what we are suggesting. 2 Isaiah has insisted vehemently on God's incomparability, yet its frail, obedient Servant of the Lord ends up elevated to quasi-divine status. The Servant unexpectedly reveals a potential within humankind for realizing the image of God, the ideal *imago Dei*. For most people, it is counterintuitive to imagine God channeling blessing to earth through a frail, marginal figure. It is unheard of among the worldly wise, but not so to those familiar with reverence theology. Those with a handle on the virtue of reverence are accustomed to such surprises from God.

At this point in our study, we are in a position to accept the thinking before us. We have already ruminated on the spirit of this theology, and hopefully come to appreciate its insights. We have wrestled with God's declaration in Isaiah 66:2, "This is the one to whom I will look, to the humble and contrite in spirit, who trembles at my word."

If divinity becomes manifest within humanity, we now know, it does so through ordinary, unlikely people like the Servant of the Lord. It appears in those who are reverently responsive to the holiness of God. God inhabits eternity, but is also present with the humble in spirit, whom he sets upright, supplies with wings, and sends soaring aloft.

Let me offer an example of how ennoblement from God may break into the human sphere among ordinary, reverent people. During World War II, in a little village in the mountains of southern France called Le Chambon, the villagers organized to rescue thousands of Jewish children and adults from starvation, exposure, deportation, and murder. They provided shelter to Jewish refugees and safe transport for them across the mountains to Switzerland. Such loving care entailed the marks true servanthood, true fidelity to the spirit of 2 Isaiah's texts. For the villagers, uplifting the weak meant sacrificial, nonviolent resistance against the strong. They chose to risk everything on the difficult path they chose, the path of other-centeredness. They knew well that the Nazis were able to destroy not only their village but also their parent body, the Protestant church of France. [2]

Biblical servanthood is a witness to God's glory, and witness is a core trait of Le Chambon's villagers. During the dark times in which they worked, the safe course would have been conformity and inactivity. Shunning cowardice and indifference, however, the villagers carried out their work of resistance in full view of their opponents. They encountered pressure and threats, but resolutely stood their ground. Many times, they disobeyed the officials and authorities.

Their life of servanthood was not so much a means to an end for the villagers, but something glorious and intrinsically valuable in itself. The Chambonnias understood their lifestyle to exhibit for all to see God's selfless love of others. It expressed God's commitment to uphold human beings as precious and uniquely irreplaceable, even at the risk to God's self of rejection, humiliation, and exposure to the greatest of dangers. Demonstrating the divine nature, God's Son gave his life on a cross for the sake of all humanity, for close friends and pitched adversaries alike. The Chambonnias felt they could answer no higher calling than living lives pointing to this divine love for the world in Christ Jesus.

The Lord vindicated their brave choice, keeping them and their denomination safe. As they lived lives of servanthood, they took to wing and soared. They displayed God's majesty on earth, not in any final, incontestable manner, but truly nonetheless. Though a mere footnote to history for the present, they shall not always remain obscure. God has surely destined them to be revealed in glory when Christ, who was their life, shows up again on this earth.

The Ancient Notion of Sacral Kingship and Its Messianic Realization

Ancient Near Eastern court symbolism formed a helpful springboard for 2 Isaiah's poetic imagination. It provided rich images of how the gods, though supreme over humanity, might display their divine majesty in human form, in the trappings of a sacral kingship. Isaiah claims God is at work to realize the noblest ideals of sacral kingship, the peace and healing of its highest aspirations.

Across the ancient Fertile Crescent, monarchs often assumed a quasi-divine status. Though mortal, they shared responsibility with the gods for such things as political and agricultural stability. Around their stable axis, their subjects and vassals prospered and flourished. They were an orienting beacon for their people, a central locus of heavenly power.

The tradition of the king as a superhuman representative of heaven appears prominently in the mythological tablets of Ugarit, a major city-state of the second millennium BCE. The people of Ugarit valued dynastic kingship as a central element of society, but considered it more than just a social institution. Kingship for them was both supernatural and divine, at least according to the witness of one of the city's mythological stories preserved on three baked-clay tablets.

Ugarit: a cosmopolitan city-state located on the Mediterranean coast of northern Syria, which flourished from about 1450–1200 BCE.

In this mythic cycle, a monarch named Kirta takes center stage. King Kirta emerges as no ordinary mortal. We read that he bears such titles as "Lad of El" (the Ugaritic high god) and "offspring of the Kind and Holy One." Such titles express Kirta's intimate, though subordinate, relationship to his divine father, "Bull El." More than just titles betray Kirta's unique identity. At his marriage, the chief god El, holding a goblet in his right hand, blesses the king in the heavenly assembly of the gods. How striking for a human to partake of such fellowship!

Hittite reliefs from around the thirteenth century BCE illustrate a similar divine-human intimacy. In these sculptures, a giant-sized god embraces and leads the Hittite king. The deity wraps his mighty arm around him and tightly clasps his hand. This is no brief contact on a special occasion, as with the blessing at Kirta's marriage. The Hittite ruler claimed divine accompaniment throughout life.

The Hittites: an ancient people of Asia Minor and Syria, whose empire reached its height in the fourteenth century BCE.

Near Eastern iconography commonly depicted kings resplendent with divine glory, standing in the place of the gods, maintaining divine order. The many names and titles of the Egyptian monarch Sahure (2480–2350 BCE), for example, crowd the space between earth and sky in the image on his tomb. The majesty of King Sahure obviously laid claim on the world and everything in it.

The same symbolism occurs in the decoration on a contemporary Egyptian comb, where the king's palace and rule dominate the cosmic order. Conspicuously, the emblems of the king take the traditional place of the sun god on this representation. Like the sun god, the king is a brilliant lord and a household name.

Ancient Near Easterners expected the beneficial sovereignty of an ideal king to encompass all peoples. They expected it to put down all that was injurious, hold war in check throughout earth's lands, and liberate the world's oppressed peoples. Indeed, a monarch's reign of justice and peace could not be ideal, they believed, unless it had a truly cosmic sweep.

Consider, for example, the image of royal triumph on a carved ivory from Canaanite Megiddo (1350–1150 BCE). Cherubim statues flank Megiddo's king, representing his numinous wisdom, might, and speed. A spirit of holiness informs and empowers his rule, the scene suggests. Birds fly from his throne room, spreading word of his glorification to the four quarters of the world. All nations should share in the king's victory celebration and prepare to enjoy its benefits.

Megiddo: an important ancient city of northern Palestine, strategically located in the Jezreel Valley north of Samaria.

In Egyptian royal symbolism, arrows accomplish the same purpose as the birds of Megiddo's king. During his coronation, a new pharaoh would release his bow in each of the four cardinal directions, signifying the far-flung reach of his power and authority. In a relief from Karnak (fifteenth century BCE), the god Seth prominently steadies the Egyptian king as he draws his bowstring as part of such a coronation.

Attracted to an ideal king's light and glory, the world's peoples get excited, rise up, and come together. Their flurry of activity, mounting joy, and newly kindled reverence is abundantly apparent in a wall relief from a tomb at Amarna (fourteenth century BCE). The Egyptian king, Amenophis IV, sits enthroned in the relief's center amid a multitude of registers. Scene upon scene is packed with envoys from earth's nations. Some bear presents: gold from the south, chariots and horses from the north, ostrich plumes and eggs from the desert dwellers. The atmosphere is at once sacred and festive. Animals from the royal zoo are present. There are exhibitions of wrestling and much joyous dancing, especially by the king's visitors from Africa. The embassies know that the king has fresh power to check the world's feuds and distribute gifts to his worldwide friends.

2 Isaiah takes ancient Near Eastern royal ideals such as these and projects them in its vision of a coming era of salvation. Its poems prophesy a royal transformation of the faithful people of God, so that they may preside over a coming messianic reign of peace. They are redeemed and beatified, in the latter chapters of our poetry, so as to truly bear divine majesty, just like King Kirta, Amenophis IV, and other idealized Near Eastern monarchs. As God's viceroys, they now represent God's power and beauty on earth.

As vicars of God, the redeemed of the Lord wear divine glory like a magnificent adornment (60:19; cf. Isa 4:2; 46:13; 52:1). They become "a crown of beauty in the hand of the LORD, and a royal diadem" (Isa 62:3). Back home at Zion, they participate in the dawning on earth of God's everlasting majesty. At that time, in those circumstances, the community of faith finally fulfills its destiny as veritable sons and daughters of God.

> The LORD will be your everlasting light, and your God will be your glory. —Isa 60:19

Like the Suffering Servant, whom they take as their model, the community of faith projects the royal attributes of the Messiah prophesied in Isaiah 11. Look closely at Isaiah's vision of the people's coming glory in Isaiah 60:21. The verse reads:

Your people shall all be righteous; /
   they shall possess the land forever. //
They are the shoot that I planted, /
   the work of my hands, so that I might be glorified. //

Note the strong verbal allusions to Isaiah's "branch of Jesse" passage. The ideal son of David in Isaiah 11 judges with "righteousness," even wearing it as a belt (Isa 11:4, 5). Just so, the members of Isaiah's messianic community shall all be fully "righteous." Just as the Messiah in Isaiah 11 is a "shoot from the stump of Jesse" (Isa 11:1), God's servants in 2 Isaiah are God's "shoot that I planted." Their shining majesty brings glory to God, just as Jesse's branch stands "as a signal to the peoples" (Isa 11:10).[3]

> On that day the root of Jesse shall stand as a signal to the peoples. —Isa 11:10

The latter idea of majesty as a beckoning signal is crucial in Isaiah. As the glory of the Lord rises upon Zion, the city's people become a beacon of witness to the world. Transformed into true vicars of God, Israel magnetically attracts earth's nations. The poems of 2 Isaiah have already made the notion a main concern prior to Isaiah 60:21. Isaiah 55:5 states: "Nations that do not know you shall run to you, because of the LORD your God, the Holy One of Israel, for he has glorified you." And Isaiah 60:3 proclaims: "Nations shall come to your light, and kings to the brightness of your dawn."

The expectation that God will one day show forth the divine glory through God's people fits the theology of the Reverence School. A brief glance at the core story of the Reverence School in the Pentateuch assures us of that. The overall shape of its story of salvation is one of promise awaiting fulfillment, of great expectation that is yet unrealized.

At a key moment of the story, God calls Abraham to become the nations' spiritual "father"—their guiding model (Gen 17:4–5 RS). God promises to vest Abraham's descendants with an everlasting covenant, a covenant not merely internal to Israel. God's chosen people must bear it visibly upon God's land amid the peoples of the earth (Gen 17:7–8 RS). They must be a beckoning signal to all nations (see especially Ps 47:9).

115

Unfortunately, the Pentateuch ends with Israel outside the land, their ideal signal-light veiled. Upon reconnoitering the promised land, God's people, the escapees from Egypt, turn back in fear and rebellion (Num 14). The exodus and wilderness wanderings end with settlement in God's land an unrealized goal. The realization of God's promises must wait for a future generation, according to the Reverence School. At the close of the Pentateuch, the people are not yet established as a community of witnesses to God's glory.

Now, at the time of 2 Isaiah's poems, the question of when this might happen is reopened. In Babylonia, the people find themselves out of the land, dispirited, and yet challenged to envision a wholly different destiny by the narratives of their Reverence School Scriptures. The magnificent poetry of 2 Isaiah announces to this people the imminent realization of Scripture's goals. God will now use them to get glory, thus transforming our broken world. God's word now shows itself indefatigable, invincible. 2 Isaiah's poems proclaim God's fulfillment of all the covenantal commitments set forth in the Scriptures of the Reverence School. In their words of prophetic fulfillment, the divine promises of the past finally bear their fruit.

The Idea of Majesty in the Reverence School

God's awesome majesty is central to the larger school of priestly theology to which 2 Isaiah belongs, the Reverence School. Indeed, the poetic texts of Isaiah lean on and draw out the royal symbols of this source of the Pentateuch, as I shall show.

In the theology of the Reverence School, God's desire is to be honored as cosmic king by all flesh (Exod 8:19; 14:17 RS). Far from divine egoism, this is God's provision to liberate us from our prideful ambition to manipulate the world, which has been damning us. At history's climax, God will move incontestably to establish divine sovereignty over creation. For the time being, however, God's majesty is largely hidden from our profane, violent world.

God's glory has not completely abandoned earth, even with all its brokenness. Rather, it reveals itself in ways that make human reverence and hope possible. Most often, divine majesty is manifest in one of three rather different ways.

First, within the accounts of the Reverence Scriptures, God's glory makes striking appearances at the wilderness tabernacle and Jerusalem's temple. There, the heavenly king has an earthly throne: the dais of the ark of the covenant. The divine glory is overpowering and unapproachable; thus, it appears at the ark only intermittently. Such appearances are "like a devouring fire," deadly even for an Israelite priest (Exod 24:17; Lev 9:23–24 RS). In Leviticus 16, God instructs Moses to "tell your brother Aaron not to come just at any time into the sanctuary . . . or he will die; for I appear in the cloud upon the mercy seat" (v. 2 RS). Both priests and people must glimpse God's majesty briefly and only with adequate preparation.

The second way that God's majesty manifests itself emerges plainly in the Reverence School's creation account in Genesis 1. There, at verse 26, God creates humankind in the image of God. "Let us make humankind in our image," God declares, "according to our likeness; and let them have dominion." From the start, the Lord wanted humanity to image the majesty of God. The Lord intended us to rule as regents, with "dominion" over earthly life. Blessed with a sort of sacral kingship, we were to bear responsibility for earth itself.

No one stands a chance of challenging God's glory and majesty—who even comes close to being like God? (Gen 1:1; Isa 40:18; 44:7–8). Yet, God chooses to appoint delegates who reveal God's royal beauty within creation. The Lord of nature's spheres stands beyond all creatures' reach, but uses agents to allow those here on earth to experience the divine person and purpose. These agents share God's royal splendor, bearing God's image: the *imago Dei* (Gen 1:26–28). The *imago Dei* gives one a royal status, an uncanny aura of dominion that all creation necessarily respects (Gen 9:2, 6–7).

This wonder does not contradict a transcendent, non-anthropomorphic view of God. Rather, it reinforces it. In designating humanity as God's image, God elevates the unlikely and humble—namely, frail humanity—to a royal status, which redounds to God's praise as the unfathomable one. Psalm 8 explicitly illustrates this dynamic, tracing how God's elevation of lowly humanity leads directly to praise of God. The poem declares, "What are human beings that you spare a thought for them? . . . Yet you have made him little less than a god, you have crowned him. . . . Yahweh our Lord, how majestic your name throughout the world!" (vv. 4–5, 9, NJB).

In designating humanity as God's image, God elevates the unlikely and humble—namely, frail humanity—to a royal status, which redounds to God's praise as the unfathomable one.

A desire for bestial slaves is the gods' purpose for men and women in parallel Near Eastern creation accounts, but Genesis 1 (RS) goes in a different direction. Rejecting anthropomorphic theology, it discards the idea of needy deities requiring servile menials. The biblical God endows humans with royal traits. God creates them "in the image of God" (Gen 1:27) to be God's royal representatives on earth, an ideal that Genesis 17 (RS) describes as finally taking root, in God's time, among Abraham's people. When God focuses on Abraham in Genesis 17, according to the Reverence School, it is a plan to fulfill the ancient divine will to use humanity to bless and guard the earth. Genesis 17 promises Abraham will be "fruitful" (v. 6) and "multiply" (v. 2), fulfilling the specific divine intentions staked out in Genesis 1:27–28.[4]

2 Isaiah exhorts its readers to embody their identity as progeny of Abraham, whom God blessed and multiplied (Isa 51:2). Like Abraham, they are frail and transient, but God has appointed them to become channels of God's power. Sacral kingship is their God-determined destiny. The image of God is linked to "dominion" according to Genesis 1:28, and Abraham is to take up this dominion. Like King David, "a witness to the peoples, a leader and commander for the peoples" (Isa 55:4), Abraham is to put on God's magnetic glory like a crown. He is to put God's majesty on display, become a spiritual *father* of earth's nations (Gen 17:4–5). So are his descendants, the people of Israel, according to 2 Isaiah. Like their ancestor of old, they should become a beacon of splendor for earth's peoples (Isa 55:4–5). Glorified in the reign of God, they should summon all the earth's princes for worship as "the people of the God of Abraham" (see Ps 47:9).

Divine majesty can become manifest on earth in a third and final way. The Reverence School and related Scriptures held that Judah's kings could embody divine majesty, just as King Kirta did. According to the Reverence School, God chose the line of David to mold it into a highly concentrated instance of God's grant of royalty to Abraham's people.

Several psalms link Davidic kingship to God's earlier Abrahamic covenant. Psalm 72:17, for example, gives the Davidic monarch Abraham's exact assurance by God: all the families of the earth would be blessed in him (Gen 12:3; 22:18). In like manner, Psalm 101:2 directs Judah's king back to Abraham's model. It holds him responsible to the particular ideal of "integrity" ("blamelessness") specified in Abraham's covenant (Gen 17:1).

Such psalms have a good warrant for connecting Israelite kingship with Abraham. A promise of unique monarchs for Judah is in fact central to God's assurances to the ancestor in Genesis 17. "Kings will come forth from you," God declares to him (Gen 17:6 RS). Both Sarah and Jacob found themselves oriented to the same divine pledge (Gen 17:16; 35:11 RS). From the start of God's relationship with Israel, back in the Genesis era, God intended to share regal power with a definite dynasty of Israelite kings. Psalm 72 and Psalm 101 unambiguously attest to this theme.

The Problem of Davidic Royalty in 2 Isaiah

Scholars have long recognized the presence in 2 Isaiah's texts of symbols of ancient Near Eastern sacral kingship. The language of Zion, David's royal city, firm amid a tottering cosmos directly informs Isaiah 54:10 (cf. Ps 46). Royal language about a coming righteous reign of a shoot of Jesse makes a strong showing in Isaiah 53:2 and 60:21 (cf. Isa 11:1, 4).

Students of Isaiah have considered this mostly routine, for other Scriptures such as the Psalms regularly use such symbolism. What has appeared remarkable is how little 2 Isaiah has to say overtly about King David himself and David's royal line. We get provocative allusions to David's father Jesse and a tender messianic "shoot," but 2 Isaiah names David only once, in Isaiah 55:3. The same verse contains our only direct mention of God's special covenant with David in 2 Samuel 7.

In his Anchor Bible commentary on Isaiah, Joseph Blenkinsopp remarks: "A striking feature of Isa 40–66 is that nowhere in the aspirations for and dreams of a future restoration is there place for *the monarchy*." Later, commenting on Isaiah 62:1–5, he makes note of the passage's "apparently complete lack of interest in the restoration of the native dynasty," where in a similar passage elsewhere in Scripture this might well be expected.[5] In 2 Isaiah, God's royal vicar is first and most obviously the faithful community as a whole, not an individual messianic king. Many biblical texts specifically celebrate Davidic royalty and David's royal descendants, not a general royalty of Israel, so this has seemed puzzling.

A popular view holds that we find in 2 Isaiah nothing short of a radical new departure. In the face of disappointment or disillusionment with Davidic kingship, the texts have "democratized" Israel's messianism. That is, after years of painful experience with an inept and oppressive Davidic dynasty, the texts have shifted their understanding of Israel's royal covenant away from David's specific line of progeny. Instead, God will realize the divine purposes for the world through the entire sacral community.[6]

This understanding of 2 Isaiah misconstrues its meaning. In particular, it fails to grasp the roots of Isaiah's theology in earlier biblical sources. 2 Isaiah's thinking on royalty in Israel does not arise *ex nihilo*, but out of the Scriptures of the Reverence School. They contain the clues for understanding how the Isaiah community was able to take royal theology in the direction that it does.

Ruminating on Isaiah 55:1–5

Isaiah 55:1–5, where alone in 2 Isaiah David is named, is the Scripture most scholars rely on to argue that our poems have democratized Israel's messianism. A close look at this text, however, reveals no democratizing at all, but thoughtful echoes of Reverence Scriptures in Genesis and their particular brand of royal thinking.

[1] Ho, everyone who thirsts, come to the waters; /
   and you that have no money, //
come, buy and eat! /
   Come, buy wine and milk /
   without money and without price. //
[2] Why do you spend your money for that which is not bread, /
   and your labor for that which does not satisfy? //
Listen carefully to me, and eat what is good, /
   and delight yourselves in rich food. //
[3] Incline your ear, and come to me; /

listen, so that you may live. //
I will make with you an everlasting covenant, /
    my steadfast, sure love for David. //
⁴ See, I made him a witness to the peoples, /
    a leader and commander for the peoples. //
⁵ See, you shall call nations that you do not know, /
    and nations that do not know you shall run to you, //
because of the LORD your God, /
    the Holy One of Israel, /
    for he has glorified you. //

Inviting metaphors abound as the poem begins, immediately drawing readers' interests. Then, the metaphors give way to a specific vision of joy. By verse 5, we understand in concrete terms the spectacular thrust of this triumphant text. In joyful delight, the passage is proclaiming God's will to shed royal glory on the entire community of faith. God has a plan for the direction of history, and our sacral ennoblement as God's own people is the specific end in mind.

The advent of divine royalty among the people of God will give them a magnetic attractiveness, provoking the fascination of far-flung nations. "Nations that do not know you shall run to you" (v. 5). Those who do not yet know God or pay attention to the community of faith will now take notice, coming to a new cognizance of their identity. Recognizing the faith community as God's own company of friends by means of their dawning new majesty, whole peoples of the globe will run to join in their fellowship.

> The advent of divine royalty among the people of God will give them a magnetic attractiveness, provoking the fascination of far-flung nations.

Sacral kingship for God's people is the theme of our poem, the kind of holy majesty that God, in "steadfast, sure love," granted to King David. Verses 3–4 state this unequivocally, proclaiming the imminent establishment of David's royal covenant, the covenant promised to him back in the era when monarchy first emerged in Israel (2 Sam 7). The blessings compacted through God's everlasting covenant with David must, our passage asserts, now blossom in full flower on earth.

Profound spiritual nourishment is close enough to grasp, the poem announces in its opening verses. God's plans for exiled Israel do not stop at a political repatriation of Zion's lost children. God is making available the power-laden nutrients for humankind's full flowering into its ultimate spiritual stature. The texts of 2 Isaiah are about humanity's ultimate destiny, not merely a moment of grace within Israel's ancient history.

Isaiah 55 uses almost the exact wording found in Ps 89:49, proclaiming the Davidic covenant relevant to the Israelite people as a whole. It goes farther, however, speaking of all Israel's people as themselves royal kings. God states, "I will make with *you all* [the Hebrew is plural] an everlasting covenant, / my steadfast, sure love for David //" (v. 3).

It is perfectly understandable that past interpreters have turned to texts specifically about Davidic kings in trying to illuminate the background of our passage, texts such as 2 Samuel 7:4–17 and Psalms 2 and 110. 2 Samuel 7 contains Scripture's prime description of the Davidic covenant, recounting Nathan's foundational prophecy of God's unilateral and unconditional support of David and his line. Psalms 2 and 110 describe Davidic kings as God's begotten sons (Ps 2:7)—priestly mediators of God's power (Ps 110:4). Interpreters who stop with these texts in Samuel and Psalms, however, fail to grasp the theology of Isaiah 55. 2 Isaiah's understanding of sacral kinship interconnects with a more expansive, inclusive royal theology. In this theological perspective, God's grant of royal blessing reaches out beyond David's dynasty to encompass the entire family of God.

Several details within Isaiah 55 betray the affinity that I am suggesting. To start, consider the idea in verse 5 of Israel as a spiritual beacon to the nations. Reverence School texts of Genesis have just this notion, identifying Abraham, Sarah, Jacob, and their descendants as guiding beacons for the peoples of the world. In Genesis, God appoints Abraham a spiritual "father" and mentor to earth's people (Gen 17:4–5). This "fatherhood" entails his becoming a veritable light to the nations, not the idea suggested by some interpreters that a few nations such as the Ishmaelites and the Midianites would trace their ancestry from him. Abraham did sire the Ishmaelites and the Midianites, but that fact is not relevant here. The Reverence School emphasizes that both Sarah and Jacob also bore God's promise of parenting nations (Gen 17:16; 35:11). This forces us to accept a spiritual meaning in understanding Abraham's status as a "father." Sarah is not related to the Ishmaelites or Midianites, and Jacob sired no other nation than Israel.

The wording of Genesis 35:11 further supports the argument, pushing us toward a spiritual understanding of the fatherhood of the ancestors. It prophesies that Jacob will bring into being an "assembly of nations," conjuring a specific picture of the patriarch's destiny. If these terms mean here what they do elsewhere in Scripture, the passage foretells that Jacob will one day convene an international congregation for worship (cf. Deut 5:22: Ps 107:32; 2 Chr 20:5; Joel 2:16). Later interpreters of Genesis 35, such as the writers of Isaiah, found this picture a clear mandate for international leadership and witness. The people of Jacob are to be royal vicars of the Lord, leading earth's nations in the liturgical service of God.

The term "everlasting covenant" in Isaiah 55:3 catches our eye, since it is most familiar to students of the Bible from Genesis 9:16 and 17:7, 13, 19. These are pivotal passages of the Reverence School, relating the story of God's earliest covenants enacted as primeval divine efforts to bless humanity. These covenantal texts have profoundly royal dimensions.

For 2 Isaiah, the present era is witnessing the redemption of divine promises made during the Genesis era (see Isa 41:8; 51:2), eternal promises independent of the Sinai covenant and Israel's history under the Davidic monarchs. Such promises even the unfaithfulness of Israel during its history in the land had no power to dissolve.

> Look to Abraham your father and to Sarah who bore you; for he was but one when I called him, but I blessed him and made him many.
> —Isa 51:2

In particular, Genesis 17 anticipates Isaiah 55's vision of an expansive, inclusive sacral kingship on earth. It presents Abraham and Sarah as a royal couple, vicars of God in the world. David's regal existence was removed from an everyday lifestyle but Abraham and Sarah, by contrast, are a couple to whom everyone can relate. All the faithful look to them as ancestors (cf. Isa 51:2). They exemplify how ordinary, frail people may be key players in God's plans.

Long before David, according to Genesis 17, God elevated Abraham to royal status and made all his seed—not just a single dynasty—beneficiaries of an "everlasting covenant" (Gen 17:7; Isa 55:3). There was ready potential in this Reverence tradition for the authors of 2 Isaiah to apply the promises of God's royal covenant to God's people as a whole. They had no need to resort to innovation and creativity, no need to "democratize" the Davidic covenant.

God addresses Abraham in royal terms in Genesis 17, signaling that Abraham himself is as much a monarch as King David. In particular, the language of Genesis 17:1 turns up elsewhere in Scripture in passages relevant specifically to David's line. Thus, 1 Kings 3:6 speaks of King David in the very terms of Genesis 17:1, and God addresses King Solomon in 1 Kings 9:4 in just the same way. Moreover, King Hezekiah in Isaiah 38:3 assumes that comparable language is relevant to him. Echoing Abraham's traits, he claims to have "walked" before God "in faithfulness with a whole heart."

The notion is striking. Abraham displays the magnetic, divine royalty of a begotten son of God that also finds expression in Scriptures about the Davidic line of kings that arose long after him (cf. Ps 72:8–11; 89:27). Back behind David stands Abraham, an ideal divine son. He stands in possession of a divine blessing powerful enough to attract the reverence of the nations.

I conclude that the faith community may inherit God's "steadfast sure love for David" simply by living into the Abrahamic covenant of Genesis 17, which God established long before Israel ever assembled as a nation at Mount Sinai. A royal covenant already applies to all those who number themselves among the spiritual descendants of Abraham and Sarah. Abraham represented pristine, archetypal Davidic royalty—Davidic royalty *in nuce*. Here is an established, scriptural warrant for the poetic image of Isaiah 55:3.

> A royal covenant already applies to all those who number themselves among the spiritual descendants of Abraham and Sarah.

Based on Reverence School tradition, 2 Isaiah's authors rightly call David "a leader and commander for the peoples" (Isa 55:4). They have solid precedent as well, however, for calling all readers of the book, even "commoners" such as ourselves, to prepare for a royal vocation as vicars of God. Readers should model themselves after Abraham and Sarah (Isa 41:8; 51:2; 54:1–2), believing that the blessings of royalty promised in Genesis are about to come showering into their lives (Isa 48:19; 54:3).

Our passage in Isaiah 55 believes that the divine work begun with Israel's earliest progenitors is about to find fulfillment as each reader becomes a "witness to the peoples," just as Abraham and Sarah were destined to be. We may be sure that the texts of Isaiah 40–66 have little patience for any reader who insists on hiding his or her light under a bushel, shunning God's call for the faithful to aspire to be spiritual models and leaders on earth.

Ruminating on Isaiah 65:23b–25

Isaiah 65:23b–25 sums up and drives home the themes we have been discussing. It inspires us with a contagious vision of future human majesty. Sometime soon, according to the poem, we, as God's true vicars, will preside over a messianic reign of peace on earth.

> 23b For they shall be offspring blessed by the LORD— /
>   and their descendants as well. //
> 24 Before they call I will answer, /
>   while they are yet speaking I will hear. //
> 25 The wolf and the lamb shall feed together, /
>   the lion shall eat straw like the ox; /
>   but the serpent—its food shall be dust! //
> They shall not hurt or destroy /
>   on all my holy mountain, //
>   says the LORD. //

The poem elicits tears of joy: the fulfillment of God's will for creation is taking shape. Earth's chaos and violence are about to become past history, things all but forgotten. In their place is coming blessing and shalom, reverence and majesty. Isaiah 65 is joyfully messianic, revealing God's coming reign of peace.

Glance for a moment at the contents of verse 25. As clear as day, the verse looks forward to the messianic era. It is under the care of the Branch of Jesse that "the lion shall eat straw like the ox" (cf. Isa 11:7). It is during the messianic reign that "they shall not hurt or destroy on all my holy mountain" (cf. Isa 11:9). Only then do the meek of the earth find equity, the world's nations, harmony.

Whereas Isaiah 11 speaks overtly of an individual Messiah, Isaiah 65 shifts our focus. Instead of chapter 11's bare image of a messianic "branch," it pans out to reveal the branch's many buds. Messianism in our poem is vibrant and fecund, *budding* with new growth. This is a vision of messianism spreading communally. Our poem's authors are pushing their readers to take up as a group the role of God's royal steward.

> Messianism in our poem is vibrant and fecund, budding with new growth. This is a vision of messianism spreading communally.

By this point in 2 Isaiah, the Servant of the Lord has done his work. Isaiah 53 is twelve chapters back. Now, it is time for those who embrace his pattern of life to take center stage. Our poets look forward to an entire community of servant-regents serving God on God's earth. In our individualistic times, it is often jarring to feel the Bible's relentless tug to get us thinking communally. Community, however, is the biblical means by which salvation comes to the world. Salvation's meaning and goal is also community, that is, mutuality within the human family.

Identifying its audience as "offspring blessed by the LORD" (65:23), our passage virtually proclaims its hearers' royalty. The same phrase appears a few chapters earlier, in Isaiah 61:8–10, where "offspring" receive an "everlasting covenant" from God. This is the covenant that Isaiah 55 has emphasized. When we are faced with poetic language about *blessed offspring,* we must hear these resonances. We must call to mind those who are inheriting God's royal covenant with Israel, God's steadfast, sure love for David (55:3).

In Judah's past, David's dynasty was bogged down in mundane politics, stifled by fear and pride. It simply could not rise to its God-willed destiny. Here, in our poem, Israel's royal covenant bursts beyond its earlier handicaps; it springs up before the world in right ways and contagious praise. Now, God and God's people are so attuned to one another, God knows their inner thoughts and instantly meets their unspoken needs (v. 24). Now, God's people become "known among the nations" (61:9), recognized by the world as channels of God's blessing.

Language about a chosen group of "offspring" is not new with our poem (see Isa 61:9), not even new with the writing of the book of Isaiah. It traces all the way back to Genesis 17 (RS). In the Pentateuch, it figures explicitly in Abraham's royal covenant. God never intended Abraham to be the lone bearer on earth of the role of divine vicar. He was a principal party to God's royal covenant, but so also was his "offspring" or "seed."

God specifically stated to Abraham, "I will establish my covenant between me and you, and your *offspring* after you throughout their generations" (emphasis added). God promised to make this "an ever-lasting covenant"; the Lord solemnly committed "to be God to you and to your offspring after you" (Gen 17:7). In Abraham's person, then, God established a firm beachhead for vesting divine majesty within humanity. That was a starting point for working toward God's ultimate goal: forming an entire royal community of servants of the Lord. The formation of this community has one focused purpose: to represent God's rule and blessing on the earth.

As we chew on Scripture and track down its poetic allusions, we discover ever more to delight and surprise us. Attending to detail, we find unanticipated parallels between Isaiah's Suffering Servant and Israel's frail old ancestor Abraham. In Isaiah's Servant of the Lord, God renews the very patterns of blessing begun so long ago in Genesis in the person of Israel's first progenitor. Just as with Abraham, Isaiah's Servant bears divine majesty in a preparatory, inceptive manner. The Servant's role is divine vicar—"light to the nations"—but he does not exhaust the task. He is the first exemplar of a new form of life on earth—the firstborn son, the one leading the parade. The Servant models the image of God for Israel, showing it the way, because it is not yet prepared for the challenge (Isa 40:27; 49:14). He lays before us a perfect illustration of divinely ennobled living. He embodies for us God's image, in a manner that God always intended.

As God promised *offspring* to Abraham, so Isaiah's Servant receives this blessing. God is making his life an offering for sin, Isaiah 53:10 declares, and from his self-sacrifice the Servant will see seed come forth—life, life, and more life. This "seed" or "offspring" is the very thing spoken of in our poem. Isaiah 65 connects back to the fourth Servant Song and, through it, back to God's royal covenant with Abraham. As Yale's Brevard S. Childs states well: "The link with the promise to the Suffering Servant is fully evident: 'He shall see offspring. . . . From the agony of his soul he will see.'"[7]

> When you make his life an offering for sin, he shall see his offspring. —Isa 53:10

Isaiah 65 is proclaiming the triumph of God's promise of off-spring to Abraham, God's promise of offspring to the Suffering Servant. In the prophetic vision of our poem, the Servant has spawned an entire community of divine vicars on earth. As of Isaiah 53:10, and throughout the rest of the book of Isaiah, the one Servant of the Lord suddenly becomes a plural entity, the "servants" (Isa 54:17). This entity—God's servant community—is the group receiving David's "everlasting covenant" in Isaiah 55. Its members are the "off-spring blessed by the LORD" (Isa 61:9), who experience the messianic kingdom on God's holy mountain in our poem (Isa 65:23b–25).

Like Abraham (Gen 17:1), the Suffering Servant is blameless, full of integrity. He paradoxically bears royalty in a humble, frail manner. He blesses those around him, not through any authority and might of his own, but by wondrously embodying God's saving power and vindication. It is no wonder, then, that as a true, ideal Abraham, he births "offspring" or "seed" on Zion. They fulfill God's purpose to bless creation, a purpose laid out plainly in the Scriptures of the Reverence School.

The heart of 2 Isaiah, and the core story of the Reverence School in the Pentateuch, is a promise of wonder for a time in the future. It is about hope: hope for a time when readers will truly occupy, finally and permanently, the privileged position of witnesses of God. God is going to establish them as a beacon of witness summoning all nations to revere the mysterious majesty of God's person.

People in the pews of today's churches often forget—and are too little reminded by those who should know better—about their place in God's revolutionary plans for human history. Although it is difficult for us to imagine it, our commonplace, modest communal fellowship in the church is God's *leaven* through which God's reign on earth must eventually take hold. God has chosen to show forth the divine glory in no other way than through the servant-hood-majesty of God's people (Isa 44:23).

> He reveals his splendor through Israel. —Isa 44:23 NET

These truths give us new direction and renewed energy. They call into question the secular reality so firmly entrenched round about us. The faith upheld in 2 Isaiah points to a new reality, one that con-tradicts the sure claims and noisy demands of secular life. The faithful must stand up for the coming new reality of God. We must summon the courage to witness to it through our actions and lifestyles as well as through our words.

> Grant us, Lord, not to be anxious about earthly things, but to love things heavenly; and even now, while we are placed among things that are passing away, to hold fast to those that shall endure. (Episcopal *Book of Common Prayer,* Collect for Proper 20)

Impetus and courage for bearing witness to God's true reality—the things "that shall endure"—is 2 Isaiah's gift to its readers. Those who commit themselves to this Scripture, spending time close to its words, inevitably experience life and relate to others in ways attuned to God's dawning majesty. Let us take up our poems in this spirit, with hearty thanks offered to our Lord.

Continuing the Conversation . . .

For a complete account of the story of Le Chambon, see Philip P. Hallie, *Lest Innocent Blood Be Shed: The Story of the Village of Le Chambon and How Goodness Happened There* (New York: Harper & Row, 1979).

For further study of royal symbolism and sacral kingship in the ancient Near East, a great place to start, with plenty of illustrations, is Othmar Keel, *The Symbolism of the Biblical World: Ancient Near Eastern Iconography and the Book of Psalms,* translated by T. Hallett (Winona Lake, Ind.: Eisenbrauns, 1997).

For more on how 2 Isaiah's Servant transfers his righteousness and mission to a plurality of "servants," his "offspring," see the seminal article of W. A. M. Beauken, "The Main Theme of Trito-Isaiah: 'The Servants of YHWH,'" *Journal for the Study of the Old Testament* 47 (1990): 67–87.

ACKNOWLEDGMENTS

I would like to reiterate the deep indebtedness to my teachers that I expressed in the autobiographical note at the start of this volume, inspirational professors such as Theodore Mauch, John Gettier, Brevard Childs, Robert Wilson, and R. Lansing Hicks. Back in 2 Isaiah class in the 1980s, Ted Mauch encouraged me to write a book explaining Isaiah 40–66 one day. With a wink and a smile, he would interrupt class to insist that I jot down this or that special insight he really wanted me to include. Dr. Mauch, I hope a bit of your wisdom finds a broader audience through this volume!

I gratefully acknowledge my home institution, Virginia Theological Seminary, for encouraging and funding my research and writing. Special support for this project came from the seminary's Suzanne F. Thomas Faculty Research Award, which I received in 2006. I thank and applaud seminary trustee Dr. Will Thomas and his beloved family for establishing this award to support faculty publication. My research on this project was greatly facilitated by the librarians at our seminary's Bishop Payne Library, who were especially helpful in every respect. And I certainly acknowledge my indebtedness to my students who have studied 2 Isaiah with me, allowed me to test my ideas on them, and taught me so much. I especially thank the Reverend Stuart Shelby, an alumnus of one of my Isaiah classes, whose artwork—produced in partial fulfillment of course requirements—graces the cover of this volume.

I want to thank the Rev. Dr. Frederick W. Schmidt, series editor, and the board of the Anglican Association of Biblical Scholars for inviting me to undertake this project. The folks at Morehouse Publishing, and at their parent body Church Publishing, have been terrific to work with. I owe special warm thanks to Nancy Fitzgerald, publisher of this series, for her direction and personal support. Cynthia L. Shattuck provided invaluable counsel and help with writing. Ryan Masteller, production manager and managing editor, saw this work through to publication. I certainly also appreciate the thoughtful and thought-provoking study questions created for this volume by the Reverend Helen McPeak.

Of course, my profoundest thanks go to my closest companions and deepest friends on this earth, my wife Catherine Elizabeth and my two-year-old daughter Rebecca Ketziah. They are the reason I lift my head off the pillow each morning, and I cannot imagine life without them. You two are intensely loved!

STUDY QUESTIONS

Paula Franck

In his analysis of 2 Isaiah, Stephen L. Cook develops the themes of the radical mystery and otherness of God; servanthood for the sake of others; and the imperative to bear witness to God's majesty. Throughout the book, he emphasizes the impact of the priestly source of the Pentateuch on Isaiah's prophecies. His reverence and awe for the beauty of the language of 2 Isaiah enables readers to explore the depths and richness of the prophet's vision as "an inspired revealed witness to the reality of God." (p. xiii).

Introduction

This study guide is intended to provide questions leading to further reflection on the major ideas in each chapter. Cook provides a wealth of detailed information, so focus on those areas of most interest and explore those ideas. At the end of each session ask what captured your attention; what new insights you will take away from your discussion; and what further questions have surfaced for you.

Isaiah is one of the most influential books of the Bible. It is used more often than any of the other prophets in the lectionary, and along with the Psalms, it is the most quoted biblical book in the New Testament.

As you begin this study of 2 Isaiah, consider the following:
- What do you hope to learn?
- What are your expectations?
- What do you already know about this book of the Old Testament?
- Why are you interested in learning more about 2 Isaiah?

To get an overview, read chapters 40–66 which comprise 2 Isaiah. Read with the intention of enjoying the beauty of the language and getting an overall sense of the narrative itself.
- Isaiah contains some of the most beautiful poetry in all the world's literature. What particular images, words, etc., caught your attention?

- How would you describe the world of 2 Isaiah?
- What is God like here?
- What surprised you about the text?
- What preconceived notions were called into question?
- How were you challenged?
- What main themes did you identify in your reading?
- What does 2 Isaiah have to say to the Church and to the world?
- How does 2 Isaiah speak to you personally?

Cook notes that there is often a disconnect in our contemporary culture between rational thinking and the mystery of the Divine.

- How is this mystery of the Divine expressed in 2 Isaiah?
- What can we do to claim the sense of the holy more fully in our lives?
- What difference would it make in our personal lives as well as in the Church and the world if we could "think of God with more imagination, spiritually oriented on the *otherness* of God" (p. xvi)?

Chapter One: Second Isaiah and the Theology of Reverence

This first chapter focuses on the holiness of God and introduces us to the theology of the Reverence School. The author also provides background information about authorship of 2 Isaiah and insights into reading prophetic literature. The role of the incomparable poetry of Isaiah is emphasized throughout.

Cook begins the chapter with a warning: "To proceed farther is to put one's self and one's lifestyle of comfort at risk" (p. 2).

- What do you think Cook means when he says that we take a risk when we enter the world of 2 Isaiah?

Throughout Isaiah, God is identified as the "Holy One of Israel" with the word "holy" used in the sense of God's *otherness*—God is totally unlike anything else we know.

- How would you further describe the otherness of God?
- When have you experienced this sense of God's holiness?
- How are we to respond to this immeasurable otherness?
- How can we be in relationship with God who is totally other?

Cook also tells us that to encounter God's holiness is to experience reverence which he defines as "the capacity for awe at those things truly greater than ourselves which we cannot change, or control, or fully understand" (p. 3). Through this sense of reverence, humanity is united in mutuality and compassion with respect for the dignity of others and the wonder of nature. Reverence is the only appropriate response to God.

- When have you experienced this sense of reverence?
- How does reverence bring us finally into relationship with God and community with others?

Another characteristic of God's holiness is hiddeness: "Truly, you are a God who hides himself; O God of Israel, the Savior" (Isaiah 45:15).

- What does it mean that God is hidden?
- What is the paradox that the hiddeness of God presents to us?
- How does the hiddeness of God ultimately bring salvation?

Worship provides another way to experience the otherness of God. "When entered into with feeling, spiritual rites form a window into God's otherness" (p. 15).

- Give specific examples of how liturgy brings us into the holiness and otherness of God.
- What is the role of liturgy in our expression of reverence?
- How are we transformed by worship?

On pages 6–8, Cook describes the theology of the Reverence School.

- As you look at these characteristics, how do you see the influence of this theology in the Church today?
- What are the implications of the fact that the Reverence School avoids speaking of God in human terms?
- How then are we to describe and relate to God?
- Rather than dwelling on earth, God makes "spectacular epiphanies" in the world. Give examples of these epiphanies and their effects.
- How do you see God appearing in our world today?
- The ultimate Good News proclaimed by the Reverence School is God's promise to bless creation. What is our role in bringing about this blessing?
- The School is also based on sense of community. "Nurturing reverence requires the help of others in articulating and expressing awe" (p. 15). How does your own faith community nurture you own sense of reverence for God?

Poetry is also a vehicle for reverence. As you look at the words of 2 Isaiah, select a passage that you find particularly compelling.

- How is the awesome holiness and otherness of God that Cook describes manifested in these words?

Cook gives some guidelines for reading prophecy which he defines as "divine word channeled through human messengers, aimed at a target audience" (p. 8).

- How would you characterize the prophetic message of Isaiah, and how does Isaiah continue to speak to us today?
- Name some prophets of our own time. What is their message, and to whom is their message addressed?
- How is their message received?
- How are each of us called to be prophets?

Cook describes Isaiah as the "great communicator of the Good News of salvation in the Old Testament" (p. 6).

- What is the Good News that 2 Isaiah brings us?
- How does this Good News nurture your spiritual life?
- What evidence of this Good News do you see in the world today?

Chapter Two: The Inscrutability of God in 2 Isaiah

This chapter continues to expand on the radical otherness of God who defies human categories of rational thought.

Drawing on the work of J. B. Phillips, Cook draws the distinction between the "god of perennial grievance who forever lets us down" (p. 19) and the god of reverence.

- What are the characteristics of the god of perennial grievance as opposed to the god of reverence?
- How does belief in the god of grievances hinder our spiritual growth?
- What leads us from the god of perennial grievance to the god of reverence?

In Isaiah 42:16 we read that "I [God] will lead the blind by a road they do not know."

- How are we blind before God?
- How does our blindness ultimately lead us to God?

Cook writes that "the inscrutability of God resists our noblest attempts to capture God, even those of creeds and systematic theologies" (p. 21).

- In light of the above statement, what is the role of the creeds and theologies of the Church?

The words of Isaiah 55:8–9 eloquently capture the inscrutability of God.

- As you read these words, how would you characterize the difference between God's ways and human ways?
- In our relationship with God and with others, how can we know when we are in tune with God's ways?

The fact that God's ways differ so radically from ours also calls into question human notions of fair play as "God appears to defy all our categories of right and wrong" (p. 22). In Isaiah 45:7 God proclaims to take responsibility for the dark side of history as well as the good.

- How are we challenged by this aspect of God's inscrutability?
- How does this seeming paradox ultimately provide an answer to the injustice of the world?

Cook states that a core message of 2 Isaiah is de-selfing—putting God, not ourselves, in the center of our lives.

- How does the story told by Rudolf Otto (pp. 24–25) aid in our understanding of this decentering?
- What do we need to do in order to get outside of ourselves and make room for God?

In describing the difference between "practical spirituality" (p. 25) and the Reverence School, Cook presents further aspects of God's inscrutability.

- What is your understanding of Cook's practical spirituality?
- How do such practices influence our understanding of faith and our relationship to God?

According to the Reverence School, the temple is a place for "inarticulate awe at God's loftiness" (p. 26).

- What role does the actual space of our church buildings play in our spiritual lives?
- In what ways do our churches inspire awe of God?

Cook explains that the Reverence School focuses on *testimony* instead of *covenant*. Through testimony, worship and love to God are offered to God without expecting any further recompense.

- What are the implications of relating to God on the basis of testimony rather than covenant agreement?

Another aspect of God's inscrutability found in the theology of the Reverence School is the fact that God is revealed on earth to inspire awe.

- How is this demonstrated in the story of the hardening of Pharaoh's heart in Exodus?
- What are some of the many ways that God is revealed that inspire awe?

The role of the Persian king Cyrus in the return of the exiles to Israel further illustrates the emphasis of the Reverence School that God's ways are beyond the grasp of human rationality.

- As you read Isaiah 45:4–8, what do you learn about God and how God acts in the world to fulfill God's purposes?

- How do we account for the fact that Isaiah tells us that God is responsible for chaos and woe?
- How are we called in the passage to respond to the Lord?
- As you read the verses about the imagery of the potter and clay, what are the implications for the nation of Israel as they await liberation from exile in Babylon?
- Here Cook also calls attention to the God of aesthetics. How does beauty bring about Gods' purposes?

Cook states that for God to be God, worthy of reverence, our cherished ideas of the divine must constantly be exposed as inaccurate.

- What are some of our most closely held ideas of God that Isaiah calls into question?

Reflect on the inscrutability of God as presented here.

- How have your perceptions of God been changed and/or challenged?
- How would you describe this inscrutability?
- What is the ultimate purpose of God's inscrutability?
- How have you experienced the awesome holiness of Cook's inscrutable God?

Chapter Three: Reverence and the Collapse of Pride and Ignorance

In this chapter we see how idolatry, pride and ignorance lead to alienation from God and others. Cook shows us how the words of the prophet Isaiah provide an antidote for this estrangement.

Cook introduces two figures from C.S. Lewis' book *The Pilgrim's Regression*—Superbia, representing pride and Ignorantia, representing ignorance. Working together, these two forces pose the greatest threat to reverence.

Superbia personifies pride which in spiritual terms indicates the claim to control the mystery of the divine that is ultimately a form of idolatry.

- How do you see Superbia at work in the world today—how do we attempt to control God for our own means?

The character of Ignorantia personifies those who are overly gullible and easily put trust in false claims leading to disappointment and victimization.

- How do you see Ignorantia at work in the world?
- How does ignorance interfere with spiritual growth and relationship with God?

In attempting to control God, following in the way of Superbia leads to idolatry. Thus 2 Isaiah uses satire to mock those who build idols. Read the following passages, and discuss what the prophet has to say to us about idols: 40:18–20; 41:6–7; 44:9–20; 46:1–7.

An idol is not limited to a physical object that is the subject of worship. In broadest terms an idol can be anything that is accorded blind admiration or excessive devotion.

- Name some of the idols of our contemporary culture and how the worship of these idols interferes with our relationship with God and with others.
- What is the difference between an object of reverence and an idol?
- How can we avoid and combat idolatry in our personal lives?

Closely related to idolatry is anthropomorphism which attempts to "make God look like a creature of the earth" (p. 46).

- Think of some examples of how we anthropomorphize God.
- What are the dangers of attempting to make God in human images?

According to the Reverence School, God is not dependent upon or contingent in creation. For example, God does not eat sacrifices or dwell in a temple (66:1)—the temple is merely a meeting place. God speaks from between the cherubim of the ark and appears in clouds and fire. Thus "negative means" must be used to combat anthropomorphism.

- How can empty space best convey the ineffable mystery of God? Give examples.

Isaiah 45:18–21 and Isaiah 46:1–4 also refute anthropomorphism and idolatry. Read these passages as well as Cook's analysis beginning on page 48.

- In these passages, how is God revealed in the world—i.e. how does God relate to the created order?
- What are God's purposes for the world?
- What is the difference between idols and the actions of God as described here?
- What is the effect of the trial scene in 45:20–21?
- How is the contrast made here between God and the idols?

Cook tells us that the main point of the mockery in these passages, especially 46:1–4 is to "create an air of shame about idolatry" (p. 54), for out of this shame comes reverence.

- How does shame lead us to reverence?

Ultimately the poetry of 2 Isaiah calls us to surrender to the otherness of God who loves us unconditionally— "to find true joy reposing in God's wonder and care" (p. 56).

- Reflect on the words of Isaiah 46:4: "I will carry and will save." When have you been carried by God?
- How do we surrender ourselves to God?
- What are the obstacles to this surrender?
- How is this surrender an antidote to pride, ignorance, and idolatry?

Chapter Four: Servanthood and the Exuberance of the Holy

The words of Soren Kierkegaard set the tone for this chapter which examines true servanthood: "It is certainly true that there are some acts which the human language particularly and narrow-mindedly calls acts of charity; but in heaven it is certainly true that no act can be pleasing unless it is an act of love: sincere in its self–abnegation" (p. 60).

As you begin your discussion, brainstorm "servant" and "servanthood."

- What are the words, phrases, images, etc. that immediately come to mind?
- What is your own understanding of what it means to be a servant of the Lord?
- Give some specific examples of those who serve as models of servanthood.
- How is a servant viewed in our contemporary culture?
- When has someone else been a servant to you?
- How have you been called to be a servant for others?

Read the so-called Servant Songs of Isaiah. It is helpful to read the passages aloud as if you are praying them in the sense of what Stephen Cook refers to as "theological meditations" (p. 69). Pay particular attention to the Third Servant Song of 50:4–11.

- 42:1–4
- 49:1–6
- 50:4–11
- 52:13–53:12
- 61:1–3

These passages give us a picture of the ideal servant.

- As you reflect on these passages, what does Isaiah tell us about servanthood?
- What is the mission of the servant?

According to 2 Isaiah, a life of servanthood is the opposite of idolatry, pride and sin with sin defined as everyone turning to his or her own way (Isaiah 53:6).

- How does a life of servanthood lead us away from the alienation of sin?

Cook discusses some of the primary qualities and actions of a servant on pages 61–62.

- As you reflect on these characteristics, how do you see them manifested in the Isaiah passages above?
- How are our relationships with others and with God defined here?
- What is the role of the community in the life of a servant?
- How does a life of servanthood lead us into wholeness?
- What are some misconceptions about servanthood?

Cook emphasizes God's preferential option for the downtrodden, for it is when we are most vulnerable that we are most likely to let down our ego and concern for self and turn to God—to let God into our lives. "But this is the one to whom I will look, to the humble and contrite in spirit" (Is. 66:2).

- What enables the downtrodden to be open to experience the awe of the holy?
- When have you been vulnerable yourself?
- How have you felt God's presence during these times?
- Who are the weary and oppressed in our world today, and how are we called through the example of the servant to serve them?

Another characteristic of servanthood is self–denial and surrender to God. Cook quotes Soren Kierkegaard as saying, "God in Heaven, let me really feel my nothingness, not in order to despair over it, but in order to feel the more powerfully the greatness of Thy goodness." (p. 64).

- What does it mean to surrender ourselves to God? What are the challenges and obstacles to this surrender?
- What modern assumptions about human autonomy and self–sufficiency are put into question here?
- What is the difference between servanthood and submission?

On pages 71–82, Cook discusses servanthood in light of the theology of the Reverence School. Here we are called to be honored servants because we have been made in God's image.

- How are observance of the Sabbath, "living by manna," concern for the oppressed and strong anti-violence integral to our embrace of servanthood?

- The Third Servant Song (Isaiah 50:4–11) presents suffering as an example of the servant's commitment to nonviolence. What is the role of non-violence and those who advocate it in the world today?
- How can times of emotional and spiritual suffering be transforming in our personal lives?

God called the Persian King Cyrus to be the instrument of salvation for Israel—to release them from captivity in Babylon.
- Think of other examples of how God uses the most unlikely individuals for God's purposes.
- What are the implications of this fact?
- What does this suggest about salvation?

Cook writes that "a genuine servant lives exuberantly, called by God's name, created for God's glory" (p. 60).
- How does Cook's metaphor of the dance on page 65 exemplify this exaltation?
- When have you experienced this "dance of spirituality" yourself?
- How are we energized and set free by a life of servanthood?

Cook defines servanthood in the context of a "privileged steward, a royal confidant" and suggests that following in the way of servanthood is to speak of "apprentice theology" (p. 67).
- How are you God's apprentice?
- How are you personally called to adhere to apprentice theology in your daily life?
- How would the world be different if we were to become servants to one another as described by Isaiah?
- How are we transformed by servanthood?
- Who are some individuals who exemplify the ideal of servanthood for you?

Chapter Five: Atonement and Exuberance

Cross calls our attention to the sacrificial aspects of servanthood. Such sacrifice is necessary in a life that is oriented toward God and neighbor if we are to grow in grace and to experience the full power of divine exuberance.

This chapter begins and ends with the premise that the divine gifts of exuberance and power come from waiting for God—i.e. "waiting spirituality."
- What is it like to be in this place of waiting?
- When have you had to wait for God?
- How are we ultimately empowered and energized by this experience of waiting for God?

Read "Holy Sonnet 14" on page 85.

- What do these words by John Donne tell us about the cost and rewards of what Cross describes as "full repose in God"?
- As you reflect on your own spiritual life, what do you need to "break, blow, burn" in order to fully embrace a life of servanthood and surrender to God?

In the theology of the Reverence School, animals sacrificed at the temple died in their owner's place as stand-ins. Cross submits that viewed in this way, animal sacrifice ultimately results in human awakening and transformation similar to what Donne describes in his poem.

- The idea of ritual animal sacrifice is distinctly foreign and even offensive in our contemporary Western culture. However, on a metaphorical level, what basic principles behind the meaning of ritual sacrifice have relevance for us today?
- According to the Reverence School, what special blessings and virtues are bestowed through sacrificial rites?
- How do such sacrifices bring us into communion with God?

Read the fourth Servant Song in Isaiah 52:13–53:12 in light of Cook's discussion of the significance of ritual sacrifice in the Reverence School.

- What are the characteristics of servanthood that are exemplified by the servant in this passage?
- What was the motivation of the Servant's actions?
- In light of Cook's discussion of the transforming aspects of sacrifice, what is the ultimate purpose and result of the Servant's offering of himself?
- How do we encounter the holy in this passage?
- How is God present in the Servant's death?
- How are we healed, transformed and empowered by the Servant's ordeal?

With regard to sacrifice, E. E. Evans-Pritchard says, "What one consecrates and sacrifices is always oneself" (p. 90).

- How is this true with regard to the Suffering Servant?
- How does this truth apply to our own lives as well?
- How does atonement lead to exuberance?

Read Isaiah 40:27–31.

- How would you describe the overall theme and tone of this passage?
- How do we see God acting in the world and in our lives?
- How is spiritual transformation and empowerment expressed here?

At its core, servanthood calls us away from self.
- How does a sense of wonder and reverence enable us to overcome our innate self–centeredness and give ourselves whole–heartedly to God and others?
- How are we set free by a life of sacrifice and servanthood?

Chapter Six: The Majesty of Servanthood

Cook concludes the study of 2 Isaiah by showing how the Lord's majesty is revealed through the servant community of God's people. Here he makes the case that the royal theology of Isaiah is grounded in the Reverence School.

Brainstorm "majesty."
- What are the words, images, etc. that come to mind?
- Rudolf Otto suggests that through majesty we get a glimpse of "supernatural holiness" (107). When have you experienced this sense of majesty?
- Describe what this was like.

God granted Israel a glimpse of God's divine majesty in order that the nation could be an instrument in revealing God's majesty on earth.
- What is our role in revealing the majesty of God — i.e. being God's regents—in the world today?
- What are the responsibilities inherent in this role?

As exemplified by the Servant of Isaiah (52:13–15; 66:2), the Lord's majesty and divinity are revealed through humility and self-sacrifice. Here the incomparable awesomeness of the Lord is in radical contrast to the frailty of the Servant. Cook further illustrates this point with the example of the villagers of Chambon, France who sheltered Jews during the Nazi occupation. (p. 111).
- How would you define humility and self-sacrifice?
- How does God call us to humility and self-sacrifice in our lives?
- Think of further examples of ordinary, reverent people who reveal the "potential within humankind for realizing the image of God, the ideal *imago Dei*" (p. 110).

Isaiah uses the language and images of the Near Eastern royal court to convey a vision of a coming era of salvation and a messianic reign of peace with God's people representing God's power on earth.
- Although the language of kings and royal courts is not consistent with contemporary Western thinking, how can we relate to God in these terms?

- What kind of imagery and language might we use instead to convey the same sense?

According to the theology of the Reverence School, divine majesty is manifested in three ways: the appearances of God at the wilderness tabernacle; the creation account of Genesis 1; and God's grant of royalty to the heirs of Abraham and thus to King David (pages 116–119).

- What is the picture of God that emerges in each of these three instances?
- How is humanity regarded here?
- What is the relationship between God and humanity?
- What is divine majesty ultimately like?

Cook believes that the conventional view that God's purposes for the world will be realized through the entire sacral community because of disillusionment with the Davidic monarchy is mistaken. Citing Isaiah 55:1–5, he makes the case that the democratization of Israel's messianism—i.e. Isaiah's royal theology—comes out of the Reverence School's understanding of Genesis 17 and the promises made to Abraham, Sarah, and Jacob.

- As you read chapter 17 of Genesis, how are the promises made to Abraham and his descendants brought to fruition in Isaiah 55:1–5?
- How is Abraham the archetype of Davidic royalty?
- Isaiah 55:1–5 rejoices in the coming restoration of Israel. As you read this passage, what do you learn about the future of Israel and its people?
- How is the majesty of God proclaimed here?
- What does it mean that we are glorified by God in Isaiah 55:5?
- What do you think Cook means when he states that "the people of Jacob are to be royal vicars of the Lord, leading the earth's nations in the liturgical service of God" (p. 123)?

Although written in the context of a specific time in history, Isaiah speaks about "humanity's ultimate destiny, not merely a moment of grace within Israel's ancient history" (p. 122).

- How does this passage continue to speak to us today?
- How do God's promises for Israel continue to extend to us even now?
- How are we the spiritual descendants of Abraham and Sarah?
- What must we do to be the witnesses to the nations that God calls us to be in Isaiah 55:5?

Now that the Servant has done his work, Isaiah 65:23b–25 summarizes the themes of the future vision of human majesty.

- What is the world like in this passage—how would you characterize this vision of the future?
- What are the promises here?
- What is our role today in helping to bring about this vision?
- What is the role of the Servant in this vision of the future?
- How is the Servant a model for us?

In the prophet's vision, salvation comes to the world through community.

- What are the implications for the Church here?

Conclude your study of 2 Isaiah by reading together the Collect for Proper 20 from the *Book of Common Prayer* on page 182.

- As you reflect on this journey with 2 Isaiah, what new insights do you have?
- What questions still remain?
- What will you take away from this study?
- How have you been inspired by the mystery and awe of the poetry of the prophet Isaiah?
- How have you experienced the holy otherness of God as expressed by the prophet Isaiah?

NOTES

LIST OF BIBLE TRANSLATIONS USED:

NAB (New American Bible)

NASB (New American Standard Bible)

NET (New English Translation)

NIV (New International Version)

NJB (New Jerusalem Bible)

NJPS (*Tanakh: The Holy Scriptures: The New JPS Translation according to the Traditional Hebrew Text*)

NLT (Holy Bible, New Living Translation, second edition)

NRSV (New Revised Standard Version)

The Message

Introduction to the Series

1. David F. Ford, "The Bible, the World, and the Church I," in *The Official Report of the Lambeth Conference 1998*, ed. J. Mark Dyer et al. (Harrisburg, Pa.: Morehouse, 1999), 332.

2. For my broader understanding of authority, I am indebted to Eugene Kennedy and Sara C. Charles, *Authority: The Most Misunderstood Idea in America* (New York: Free Press, 1997).

3. William Sloan Coffin, *Credo* (Louisville: Westminster John Knox, 2003), 156.

Autobiographical Note and Introduction

1. Quoted in Roger Ferlo, *Opening the Bible*, vol. 2 of the New Church's Teaching Series (Cambridge: Cowley, 1997), 11.

2. Quoted in Ibid., 5. See also William P. Haugaard, "The Bible in the Anglican Reformation," in *Anglicanism and the Bible*, ed. F. H. Borsch (Wilton, Conn.: Morehouse Barlow, 1984), 76.

3. Karl Rahner, *Foundations of Christian Faith: An Introduction to the Idea of Christianity,* trans. W. V. Dych (New York: Crossroad, 1978), 22. I am grateful to my colleague and friend Ruthanna B. Hooke for pointing me to this reference.

4. The theology of 2 Isaiah is a central resource for the Orthodox Jewish theologian Eliezer Berkovits in his book *Faith After the Holocaust* (New York: KTAV, 1973). For discussion, see Christine Pilkington, "The Hidden God in Isaiah 45:15—A Reflection from Holocaust Theology," *Scottish Journal of Theology* 48 (1995): 285–300.

5. St. Aelred of Rievaulx, *The Mirror of Charity: The* Speculum Caritatis *of St. Aelred of Rievaulx,* trans. G. Webb and A. Walker (London: Mowbray, 1962), 6.

6. Ibid., 7.

Chapter One: Second Isaiah and the Theology of Reverence

1. Scholars often use slashes, like the ones I have added here, to help mark off the parallel sections within poetic lines of the Bible. A double slash (//) marks the end of a line. A single slash (/) marks a logical pause within the line, and is equivalent to the asterisk (*) used in the Episcopal *Book of Common Prayer* to help parishes with the public reading or chanting of the psalms.

2. From Papyrus Leiden I 350, translated by James P. Allen (*COS* 1.16:25), in *Canonical Compositions from the Biblical World,* ed. William W. Hallo, vol. 1 of *The Context of Scripture* (Leiden and Boston: E. J. Brill, 2003), 25. All references here to this hymn are to its two hundredth chapter, on Amun's transcendence.

3. Herodotus, *The History,* 1.86, in Herodotus, *The History,* trans. David Grene (Chicago and London: University of Chicago Press, 1987), 74. Compare Alfred Denis Godley, *Herodotus with an English Translation,* 4 vols., LCL (London: William Heinemann; Cambridge: Harvard University Press, 1960), 1:111–13.

4. For more on the group behind 2 Isaiah, see Joseph Blenkinsopp, *Isaiah 56–66: A New Translation with Introduction and Commentary,* Anchor Bible 19B (New York: Doubleday, 2003), 51–54, 290–301; idem., "The 'Servants of the Lord' in Third Isaiah: Profile of a Pietistic Group in the Persian Epoch," in *The Place Is Too Small for Us: The Israelite Prophets in Recent Scholarship,* ed. R. P. Gordon, Sources for Biblical and Theological Study 5 (Winona Lake, Ind.: Eisenbrauns, 1995), 392–412; Stephen L. Cook, *The Apocalyptic Literature,* Interpreting Biblical Texts (Nashville:

Abingdon, 2003), 111–18; Robert R. Wilson, "The Community of the Second Isaiah," in *Reading and Preaching the Book of Isaiah,* ed. C. Seitz (Philadelphia: Fortress, 1988), 53–70.

Chapter Two: The Inscrutability of God in 2 Isaiah

1. J. B. Phillips, *Your God Is Too Small* (New York: Macmillan, 1958), 51.
2. Jacques Ellul, *The Politics of God and the Politics of Man,* trans. G. W. Bromiley (Grand Rapids: Eerdmans, 1972), 30.
3. Rudolf Otto, *The Idea of the Holy,* trans. J. W. Harvey (London: Oxford University Press, 1923), 81.
4. From F. W. Faber's powerful nineteenth-century hymn, "Full of Glory, Full of Wonders."
5. Israel Knohl, *The Sanctuary of Silence: The Priestly Torah and the Holiness School* (Minneapolis: Fortress, 1995), 159.
6. Unfortunately, modern English translations such as the New Revised Standard Version mostly fail to capture the Hebrew sense.
7. See Graham S. Ogden, "Moses and Cyrus," *Vetus Testamentum* 28 (1978): 195–203.
8. C. S. Lewis, *A Grief Observed* (New York: Bantam Books, 1976), 35–36.

Chapter Three: Reverence and the Collapse of Pride and Ignorance

1. This and all the following quotations are from C. S. Lewis, *The Pilgrim's Regress: An Allegorical Apology for Christianity, Reason, and Romanticism* (New York: Bantam, 1943), 190–91.
2. For discussion, see Paul Woodruff, *Reverence: Renewing a Forgotten Virtue* (New York: Oxford University Press, 2001), 117–18.
3. Lewis, *The Pilgrim's Regress,* 190.
4. Ibid., 194.
5. Cf. Ralph W. Klein, *Israel in Exile: A Theological Interpretation,* Overtures to Biblical Theology (Philadelphia: Fortress, 1979), 141–42.
6. Israel Knohl, *The Sanctuary of Silence: The Priestly Torah and the Holiness School* (Minneapolis: Fortress, 1995), 132–37. A related point concerns how the Reverence School's sacrificial system lays bare the group's opposition to human pride and conceit. The system presupposes that most of Israel's sins will be inadvertent or even unconscious. Brazen offenses against God are assumed to be rare and outrageous. See Jacob Milgrom, *Leviticus 1–16: A New Translation with Introduction and Commentary,* Anchor Bible 3 (New York: Doubleday, 1991), 258.

7. Herodotus recounts one of the best-known ambiguous oracles of the ancient world (*Histories* 1.53). See Herodotus, *The Histories,* trans. A. de Sélincourt, Penguin Classics (Harmondsworth, Middlesex, England: Penguin, 1972), 60. On necromancy, cf. Isaiah 8:19–22; 29:4.

8. Klaus Baltzer, *Deutero-Isaiah: A Commentary on Isaiah 40–55,* trans. M. Kohl, Hermeneia (Minneapolis: Fortress, 2001), 247.

9. *Enuma Elish* VI.5–8, 23–42, in Victor H. Matthews and Don C. Benjamin, *Old Testament Parallels: Laws and Stories from the Ancient Near East,* rev. and expanded ed. (Mahwah, N.J.: Paulist, 1997), 16. Cf. the discussion of Klein, *Israel in Exile,* 128.

10. See Woodruff, *Reverence,* 5, 39, 47, 72, 78, 221.

11. The story of Narcissus is told by the Roman poet Ovid (d. ca. 17 CE) in his *Metamorphoses,* 3.341–510, which is available in many English translations. A popular one is Ovid, *Metamorphoses: A New Verse Translation,* trans. David A. Raeburn, Penguin Classics (London: Penguin, 2004).

Chapter Four: Servanthood and the Exuberance of the Holy

1. Perry D. LeFevre, ed., *The Prayers of Kierkegaard* (Chicago and London: University of Chicago Press, 1956), 11.

2. Aiden Wilson Tozer, *The Knowledge of the Holy: The Attributes of God, Their Meaning in the Christian Life* (New York: Harper & Row, 1961), 36–37. I have not altered the noninclusive masculine language.

3. See W. A. M. Beuken, "Does Trito-Isaiah Reject the Temple? An Intertextual Inquiry into Isa. 66.1–6," in *Intertextuality in Biblical Writings: Essays in Honour of Bas van Iersel,* ed. S. Draisma (Kampen: Kok, 1989), 57.

4. LeFevre, *Prayers of Kierkegaard,* 5.

5. See the helpful insights of Benjamin D. Sommer, *A Prophet Reads Scripture: Allusion in Isaiah 40–66* (Stanford, Calif.: Stanford University Press, 1998), 89, 91, 251 n. 54.

6. For discussion, see Paul Woodruff, *Reverence: Renewing a Forgotten Virtue* (New York: Oxford, 2001), 165, 180–84, 190, 203.

7. On the assignment of Genesis 2:3 and Numbers 28:9–10 to the Reverence School, and on the distinctive attitude toward the Sabbath in the Reverence School, see Israel Knohl, *The Sanctuary of Silence: The Priestly Torah and the Holiness School* (Minneapolis: Fortress, 1995), 14–19.

8. On how the Reverence School text of Exodus 24 mirrors the Genesis creation account, see Norbert Lohfink, *Theology of the Pentateuch: Themes of the Priestly Narrative and Deuteronomy,* trans. L. Maloney (Minneapolis:

Fortress, 1994), 130. On the identification of Exodus 24:15–18 as Reverence School, see Knohl, *Sanctuary of Silence,* 127.

9. For discussion, see Lohfink, *Theology of the Pentateuch,* 132–33. Against Knohl, doublets and other evidence within the priestly portions of Exodus 16 betray the underlying presence of the Reverence School. The Holiness School has expanded the account, adding supplements such as verse 8 and verses 11–12, and developing the provision for the Sabbath in verses 22–30. Cf. the observations of Lohfink, *Theology of the Pentateuch,* 145; Samuel Rolles Driver, *The Book of Exodus in the Revised Version,* Cambridge Bible for Schools and Colleges (Cambridge: Cambridge University Press, 1918), 147.

10. See Lohfink, *Theology of the Pentateuch,* 127. Against Knohl, the priestly portions of Numbers 14 appear to contain material from both the Reverence School and the Holiness School. See George Buchanan Gray, *A Critical and Exegetical Commentary on Numbers,* International Critical Commentary (Edinburgh: T. & T. Clark, 1903), 4:131–32.

11. See Jacob Milgrom, *Leviticus 1–16: A New Translation with Introduction and Commentary,* Anchor Bible 3 (New York: Doubleday, 1991), 51; Walter C. Kaiser, Jr., "The Book of Leviticus: Introduction, Commentary, and Reflections," in *The New Interpreter's Bible,* ed. L. E. Keck, 13 vols. (Nashville: Abingdon, 1994), 1:1036.

12. I am referring to the picture of Abraham and Sarah in the Reverence School narrative. Other strands, of course, present less ideal portraits of the couple (e.g., cf. the J strand at Gen 12:13 and at Gen 16:4–6).

13. Author's modification of the NRSV.

Chapter Five: Atonement and Exuberance

1. Henry Sloane Coffin, "The Book of Isaiah, Chapters 40–66: Exposition," in *The Interpreter's Bible,* ed. G. A. Buttrick (Nashville: Abingdon, 1956), 5:446. Stanley's statement is from Henry M. Stanley, *The Autobiography of Sir Henry Morton Stanley,* ed. Dorothy Stanley (Boston: Houghton Mifflin, 1909), 519. The quotation from Wesley is from John Telford, ed., *The Letters of the Rev. John Wesley,* 8 vols. (London: Epworth, 1931), 7:254.

2. John Donne, *Poems of John Donne, vol. 1,* ed. E. K. Chambers (London: Lawrence & Bullen, 1896), 165.

3. See Israel Knohl, *The Sanctuary of Silence: The Priestly Torah and the Holiness School* (Minneapolis: Fortress, 1995), 33–137.

4. This will become clear in a moment, when I discuss the Reverence School thinking behind Leviticus 10 and Numbers 25, where human deaths are a completely sufficient propitiation and no animals are sacrificed. As Wen-

ham rightly notes, "Where a man died there was no need for animals to be sacrificed as well" (Gordon J. Wenham, *The Book of Leviticus*, NICOT 3 [Grand Rapids: Eerdmans, 1979], 27). Also see ibid., 109–10; Baruch A. Levine, *Leviticus: The Traditional Hebrew Text with the New JPS Translation*, JPS Torah Commentary (Philadelphia: Jewish Publication Society, 1989), xxxix, 115; Walter C. Kaiser Jr., "The Book of Leviticus: Introduction, Commentary, and Reflections," in *The New Interpreter's Bible*, ed. L. E. Keck, 13 vols. (Nashville: Abingdon, 1994), 1:999.

5. Philo Judaeus, the Hellenistic Jewish philosopher, supposed that Cain in offering God the fat of his animals was, in effect, surrendering to God "whatever there is in the soul that is cheerful, or fat, or preservative and pleasant" (*On the Sacrifices of Abel and Cain*, sec. 136).

6. For discussion, see Hartmut Gese, *Essays on Biblical Theology*, trans. K. Crim (Minneapolis: Augsburg, 1981), 114; Daniel P. Bailey, "Concepts of *Stellvertretung* in the Interpretation of Isaiah 53," in *Jesus and the Suffering Servant: Isaiah 53 and Christian Origins*, ed. W. Bellinger Jr. and W. R. Farmer (Harrisburg: Trinity Press International, 1998), 242; Kaiser, "Book of Leviticus," 1011.

7. See chapter 12, "Edward E. Evans-Pritchard (b. 1902)," in *Understanding Religious Sacrifice: A Reader*, ed. Jeffrey Carter (London and New York: Continuum, 2003), 201. For the ethnographic evidence cited in these two paragraphs, see ibid., 201–3.

8. Cited in Aiden Wilson Tozer, *The Knowledge of the Holy: The Attributes of God, Their Meaning in the Christian Life* (New York: Harper & Row, 1961), 37.

9. Jacob Milgrom, *Leviticus 1–16: A New Translation with Introduction and Commentary*, Anchor Bible 3 (New York: Doubleday, 1991), 345, 377.

10. See Patrick D. Miller, *The Religion of Ancient Israel*, Library of Ancient Israel (Louisville: Westminster John Knox, 2000), 118; Levine, *Leviticus*, 28, 33; Wenham, *Leviticus*, 110; Kaiser, "Book of Leviticus," 1038.

11. Milgrom, *Leviticus 1–16*, 332–33, 378.

12. See chapter 6, "Edward A. Westermarck (b. 1862)," in Carter, *Understanding Religious Sacrifice*, 108.

13. Ibid., 107–8.

14. Ibid., 108.

15. Rudolf Otto, *The Idea of the Holy*, trans. J. W. Harvey (London: Oxford University Press, 1923), 36–42.

16. Elaine Scarry, *On Beauty and Being Just* (Princeton: Princeton University Press, 1999), 73.

17. Longinus, *On the Sublime,* trans. with commentary by James A. Arieti and John M. Crossett, Texts and Studies in Religion 21 (New York and Toronto: Edwin Mellen, 1985), 42.

Chapter Six: The Majesty of Servanthood

1. For generalized "royal" uses of the language of "prospering," see Josh 1:7–8; 1 Sam 18:14; 1 Kgs 2:3; 2 Kgs 18:7; Pss 2:10; 101:2; Jer 3:15.
2. For a good summary of the story of Le Chambon, see George Hunsinger, *Disruptive Grace: Studies in the Theology of Karl Barth* (Grand Rapids: Eerdmans, 2000), 108–13.
3. For discussion, see Benjamin D. Sommer, *A Prophet Reads Scripture: Allusion in Isaiah 40–66* (Stanford, Calif.: Stanford University Press, 1998), 246–47.
4. Credit goes to Walter Brueggemann for realizing that this blessing intention for humanity is a core "kerygma" of the Pentateuch's priestly writings. See Walter Brueggemann, "Chapter 6: The Kerygma of the Priestly Writers," in Walter Brueggemann and Hans Walter Wolff, *The Vitality of Old Testament Traditions,* 2nd ed. (Atlanta: John Knox, 1982), 101–13.
5. Joseph Blenkinsopp, *Isaiah 56–66: A New Translation with Introduction and Commentary,* Anchor Bible 19B (New York: Doubleday, 2003), 80, 236.
6. Ibid., 80. Blenkinsopp states that in 2 Isaiah, "the Davidic covenant is *transferred* to the people as a whole" (emphasis added).
7. Brevard S. Childs, *Isaiah,* Old Testament Library (Louisville: Westminster John Knox, 2001), 538.

FURTHER READING

Paul Woodruff, *Reverence: Renewing a Forgotten Virtue*. New York: Oxford University Press, 2001. This short book is a beautifully written exposition of the virtue of reverence by an expert in classical philosophy and literature. Although it does not treat the biblical text directly, I have found in my teaching that reading this work greatly helps folks grasp the basic perspective on existence found in 2 Isaiah.

Rudolf Otto, *The Idea of the Holy*. Translated by J. W. Harvey. London: Oxford University Press, 1923. A classic of religious studies, this fulsome work is the standard treatment of the nonrational otherness of God. It illuminates a stance of reverence such as that found in 2 Isaiah in a theological and religious manner, in contrast to Paul Woodruff's philosophical and ethical approach.

Elaine Scarry, *On Beauty and Being Just*. Princeton, NJ: Princeton University Press, 1999. This deeply insightful book explores the fascinating relationship between the experience of radical beauty and the human desire for justice. Reading the work helps one begin to appreciate the link that 2 Isaiah makes between the epiphany of divine sublimity on earth and a new human consciousness of God's fairness.

Brevard S. Childs, *Isaiah*. Old Testament Library. Louisville, Kty: Westminster John Knox, 2001. Childs treats the entire book of Isaiah in one concise volume, clarifying how the present shape of the prophecy presents us with a central and compelling theological vision. The volume is packed with suggestive observations about Isaiah's literary features, theology, and history of interpretation. There is constant engagement with other critical scholarship on Isaiah.

James Muilenburg, "The Book of Isaiah, Chapters 40–66: Introduction and Exegesis." Pages 381–773 in volume 5 of *The Interpreter's Bible*. Edited by G. A. Buttrick. 12 vols. Nashville: Abingdon, 1956. Muilenburg's commentary is a classic liberal-protestant study of 2 Isaiah, best known for its astute appreciation of the form and rhetorical beauty of the prophecy. Muilenburg was the teacher of several of my professors, including Professor Mauch, whom I mention in the autobiographical note and the acknowledgments.

John N. Oswalt, *The Book of Isaiah: Chapters 40–66*. New International Commentary on the Old Testament. Grand Rapids: Eerdmans, 1998. Oswalt has written a detailed evangelical commentary full of rich theological insights. The size of the volume (over 700 pages) gives him plenty of room to unpack some of the great depth and breadth of 2 Isaiah's spiritual witness.

Joseph Blenkinsopp, *Isaiah 40–55: A New Translation with Introduction and Commentary*. Anchor Bible 19A. New York: Doubleday, 2000. This is the most up-to-date historical-critical treatment of 2 Isaiah. It is the volume to turn to for exploring the historical and social background of the prophecy and for insights into the issues involved in translating it.

ABOUT THE AUTHOR

Dr. Stephen L. Cook serves as the Catherine N. McBurney Professor of Old Testament Language and Literature at Virginia Theological Seminary, the largest of the accredited seminaries of the Episcopal Church. He and his wife Catherine, a psychotherapist, live amid the seminary community on its campus in Alexandria, Virginia, with their two-year-old daughter from China, Rebecca, who attends the campus Butterfly House preschool.

Prior to joining the VTS faculty in 1996, Stephen served on the faculty of Union Theological Seminary at Columbia University in New York City for four years. He did his doctoral training in Old Testament at Yale University after having completing the M.Div. degree at Yale's Divinity School, where he also served as an instructor and fellow. His undergraduate work was at Trinity College, Connecticut, where he graduated with honors as a religion major in 1984.

Stephen is the author of several books, including *The Apocalyptic Literature* (Abingdon, 2003); *The Social Roots of Biblical Yahwism* (Society of Biblical Literature, 2004); and *Prophecy and Apocalypticism* (Fortress, 1995). Most recently, he has written "The Season of Epiphany" in *New Proclamation Year B, 2008–2009, Advent through Holy Week* (Fortress, 2008). His other publications include journal articles, introductions and annotations to biblical books for both the *New Oxford Annotated Bible* and the *HarperCollins Study Bible*, and several entries for *The New Interpreter's Dictionary of the Bible*. He maintains a fascinating Bible Blog at www.biblische.blogspot.com.

Stephen has served in several capacities as an officer of the Society of Biblical Literature, and is currently a Regional Coordinator for the guild. He is also the Corporation Representative for Virginia Seminary to the American Schools of Oriental Research and a member of such other professional societies as the Anglican Association of Biblical Scholars and the Catholic Biblical Association. He is in high demand around the country as a lecturer, seminar speaker, and workshop leader.